THE CANADIAN
FISH COOK BOOK!

THE CANADIAN
FISH COOK! BOOK!

A. Jan Howarth

Douglas & McIntyre
Vancouver/Toronto

in co-operation with the
Department of Fisheries and Oceans
and the Canadian Government Publishing Centre,
Supply and Services Canada

Douglas & McIntyre Ltd.
1615 Venables Street
Vancouver, British Columbia
V5L 2H1

Canadian Cataloguing in Publication Data

Howarth, A. Jan, 1938-
The Canadian fish cookbook

Includes index.
ISBN 0-88894-397-0

1. Cookery (Fish) 2. Cookery (Shellfish)
3. Fishes, Dressing of. I. Title.
TX747.H69 641.6'9 C83-091188X

Design by Rick Staehling
Food photographs by Dick Lotz at Graphic Industries Ltd.
Species watercolours by Brenda Guild
Line drawings by Dick Allen
Design and original artwork of smoking kilns
   by D. G. Iredale, Fresh Water Institute, Winnipeg
Typeset by Evergreen Press
Printed and bound in Canada by D. W. Friesen & Sons Ltd.

ᥩCONTENTSᥩ

BASIC FISH COOKERY 107

RECIPES 113

To Shirley Popham

⌘PREFACE⌘

As a person who loves and appreciates fish, I have always wanted to produce a book which would give people the knowledge and ability to appreciate and love fish too. I hope this is that book. I have tried to chase the fear of the unknown out of fish preparation and replace it with helpful information, understanding and a fun approach. Fish and shellfish are easy to cook, delicious to eat and can be prepared in such an endless variety of ways that it staggers the imagination. My sincere wish is that many of the recipes and ideas will be but a starting point and will open the doors to inspirations of your own.

Thanks and acknowledgements are due to a great many people, especially in the various sections of the Department of Fisheries and Oceans. Mentioned in no particular order are the personnel in the Communication branches in both Vancouver and Ottawa, the staff of the Ottawa Fisheries Food Centre and Consumer Consultants in the various regions of Canada, particularly Newfoundland, Nova Scotia, New Brunswick and Prince Edward Island. If it sounds as though the West neglected me—I was, of course, the Consumer Consultant for Western Canada for many years. I would especially like to thank the staff at the Freshwater Institute in Winnipeg for their valuable direction regarding the species in the freshwater section and for providing me with updated information for use in the sections on the canning and smoking of fish. Thanks also go to the staff at the Nanaimo Research Station in British Columbia and the St. John's Research Station in Newfoundland for their valuable assistance regarding the species in their regions. For their tolerance of my constant pestering, my appreciation goes to the staff at the Department of Fisheries and Oceans library in Vancouver. The library was a constant and helpful reference source.

A very special thank you to all those stoic, understanding and still cheerful people in the Inspection Laboratory at 325 Howe Street, Vancouver, who did not once flinch, even when I appeared with recipe number 202 for them to taste out of the Test Kitchen. From dogfish to abalone to squid, they gave me their honest unbiased opinions, many of which changed the course of this book. An indirect offshoot of the testing of recipes leads me to also thank the man, whose name I still don't know, in the office below the Test Kitchen; he maintained a sense of humour even when, for the fifth time in a week, his office was flooded by the kitchen pipes bursting. Many, many other people, especially in the fishing industry, assisted in direct and indirect ways by helping me gain the experience and knowledge that allowed me to put this book together—to all of you, too numerous to mention—a heartfelt thanks. And last but not least, a most special thank you to my parents for their understanding and support, their patience and encouragement—to them I owe a lot.

Because of her support and encouragement to get this project underway, her consistent belief in the reasons for a book of this nature and her unyielding determination and drive which constantly opened doors for the funding that made this book possible—I dedicate this book to Shirley Popham, formerly Director of Information Services, Pacific Region, Department of Fisheries and Oceans; a good friend, who was taken prematurely and sadly will not see this finished book.

1

ABOUT FISH AND SHELLFISH

ATLANTIC SPECIES
PACIFIC SPECIES
FRESHWATER SPECIES

ABOUT FISH AND
⌾SHELLFISH⌾

The average person's knowledge of fish and shellfish is limited to a few of the better-known species such as sole, cod, salmon, halibut, crab and shrimp. Partly because of this, people tend to stick with those fish that are familiar to them and are naturally hesitant to try new ones. What often results is that these popular species, because of the laws of supply and demand, become less available and more expensive.

The glossary below, followed by descriptions of species, is the first step to an understanding of lesser-known species, all of which are quite delectable, very easy to prepare and often inexpensive sources of protein. Each species description is followed by a short note on similar species which are often interchangeable in recipes.

The next step is up to you, to take the plunge and try species which are unfamiliar to you. You will be in for a very pleasant surprise.

All the fish described in this book may be bought by consumers on the commercial market, though some may be seen more frequently than others. Many more species, too numerous to mention, are popular with sports anglers.

Groundfish (G): Fish that live, feed and are caught close to the bottom of the water.

Pelagic (P): The natural habitat of fish in this group is close to the surface in the open seas.

Anadromous (A): Fish that spend a good part of their lives in the open sea but return to rivers to spawn.

Catadromous (CAT): This group of fish lives in rivers and streams but travels out to sea to spawn.

Crustaceans (CRUST): Invertebrates that usually live in the water and breathe through gills. They have a hard outer shell, with jointed appendages and body. Crustaceans include crabs, lobsters, shrimp and prawns.

Molluscs (M): A large group of invertebrates characterized by a soft, unsegmented body enclosed, in most instances, partly or wholly in a calcareous shell of one or more pieces, and having gills, a foot and a mantle. Molluscs include oysters, clams, mussels, abalone, squid and octopus.

ATLANTIC SPECIES
FISH

ALEWIFE (CAT)

The alewife is something of a pseudo-herring, as some of its other names suggest: river herring, sawbelly, kyak, glut herring and mulhaden. This fish is also called gaspereau by the French in eastern Canada who harvest it from the Gaspereau River. The alewife has a greyish green back, with silver sides and belly. At maturity, its length is approximately 25 to 30 cm (10 to 12″), and its weight is close to 250 g (0.5 lb.). The principal harvest time is in May and June.

In recipes, alewife is interchangeable with mackerel or herring.

AMERICAN EEL (CAT)

Ranging from Greenland southward, the American eel is also called silver eel and anguille commune. It has a black to muddy brown upper body, with yellow sides and a yellowish white belly. Of elongated shape, its maximum length is 123 cm (49″), and its weight varies from 1.5 to 4 kg (3 to 9 lbs.). Although it lives much of its life in fresh water, the American eel returns to the sea to breed and is caught by traps in rivers and estuaries from August through November.

Eel has firm white flesh and a distinctive flavour. See index for preparation techniques and recipes.

AMERICAN SHAD (A)

A member of the herring family, the American shad is distinguished from the sea herring by the absence of teeth in the mouth, a thicker body and the number of lateral dark spots (always more than four). Also, the shad is larger than the herring and can reach a length of 75 cm (30″) and a maximum weight of 5 kg (11 lbs.). Otherwise, it is similar in appearance to the herring, being dark blue on the upper body and white to silver on the lower sides and belly. It is harvested during May and June in rivers and estuaries.

Shad roe is considered a delicacy and is often featured on restaurant menus. It also makes an excellent caviar (see index). The eggs are small, with a yellow-orange colour similar to that of herring roe.

In recipes, shad is interchangeable with herring or mackerel.

AMERICAN SMELT (A)

The American smelt is a small, delicate, troutlike species which belongs to the capelin family. It is also called sea smelt, rainbow smelt or sparling. Maturing at two to three years, smelt reaches from 12.5 to 20 cm (5 to 8″) in length. It is transparent olive to bottle green on the upper body, with paler sides and a silvery belly flecked with tiny dusky dots. Smelt occurs in coastal waters and is chiefly netted inshore. This fish is harvested all year, but principally during the spring spawning run and in winter months through the ice.

After cleaning, smelt is often cooked and served whole, as the bones are edible and provide a satisfying crunch. The flesh is sweet tasting.

In recipes, smelt is interchangeable with capelin or silverside.

ATLANTIC COD (G)

Atlantic cod, often referred to as "the beef of the sea," has for centuries been the backbone of the North Atlantic fisheries and the favourite fish of many nations. The average commercially caught cod weighs from 1 to 3 kg (2 to 6 lbs.), and its elongated body ranges in length from 61 to 122 cm (24 to 48″). Its natural colour varies from grey to green or brown to red, depending on its surroundings. It is capable of changing colour to match the background, though this is not a rapid changeover. The back and sides are covered with numerous brown-red spots, with a pale lateral line down the side and a familiar barbel on the chin. Cod travels in schools from deep to shallow waters in seasonal cycles and is caught throughout the year, but the principal harvest times depend on area fished, ice and weather conditions.

When cooked, cod flesh produces medium to large white flakes and is moist, with a pleasant, delicate flavour.

In recipes, cod is interchangeable with most flatfish, especially halibut, and almost all roundfish, including cusk, wolffish, hake, haddock and pollock (Boston bluefish).

ATLANTIC HALIBUT (*G*)

Halibut, the largest of the flatfish, has a large mouth and is greenish brown to dark brown on its upper, eyed side, with the blind side ranging from white to grey to a mottled grey-white. It is a remarkable fish which can vary in size from 2 to 350 kg (4 to 770 lbs.). It is graded according to weight, the average size being about 25 kg (55 lbs.). When young, it is known as chicken halibut, while the mature fish is called whale halibut. Seldom entering waters less than 60 m (200′) deep, it ranges from Labrador to the Gulf of Maine. Fishing may be conducted year round, with the principal catch being landed April through June.

One of the highest priced of commercial groundfish, halibut has a firm white flesh and a delicate, distinctive flavour.

In recipes, halibut is interchangeable with all lean firm-fleshed fish including salmon, trout, cusk, wolffish, turbot, hake, haddock and pollock (Boston bluefish).

ATLANTIC MACKEREL (*P*)

One of the pelagic species of fish, mackerel ranges over a large area of open ocean and travels mainly in schools close to the surface. Long an important food fish in many European countries, it is fast becoming better known and better accepted on this side of the Atlantic, as people turn towards more economical food buys. Mackerel is an attractive looking fish, with a steely blue upper surface marked with 20 to 23 dark wavy bars, silvery iridescent sides and a silvery white

ATLANTIC FISH

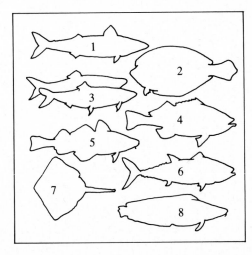

1. Atlantic mackerel
2. Summer flounder
3. Herring
4. Redfish or ocean perch
5. Atlantic cod
6. Tuna (bluefin)
7. Skate
8. Cusk

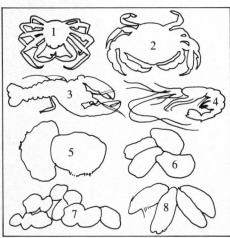

ATLANTIC AND PACIFIC SHELLFISH

1. Snow crab (Atlantic)
2. Dungeness crab (Pacific)
3. Lobster (Atlantic)
4. Pink shrimp (Atlantic)
5. Northern abalone (Pacific)
6. Oysters (Atlantic)
7. Clams: Japanese little-neck and little-neck (Pacific)
8. Blue mussels (Atlantic/Pacific)

belly. Average weight at maturity varies from 0.5 to 1 kg (1 to 2 lbs.), though it has been recorded as reaching a weight of 2 kg (4 lbs.) and a length of 55 cm (22″). It is landed principally from May through November.

In recipes, mackerel is interchangeable with herring, alewife, shad and tullibee (lake herring or cisco). Canned mackerel may be used in most recipes using canned tuna.

ATLANTIC SALMON (*A*)

A prized fish on both sides of the Atlantic Ocean, the Atlantic salmon is widely acclaimed as a gastronomic delight. Generally considered to be more akin to the trout family than to the Pacific salmon, the Atlantic salmon often lives after spawning (like trout) and may return to spawn more than once. At maturity, its length is about 75 cm (30″), and its average weight is about 4.5 kg (10 lbs.), though a few have been caught weighing over 15 kg (33 lbs.). Its colour changes with age, but is generally silvery on the sides and belly, with the upper body ranging through shades of brown, green and blue; the entire body is covered with dark crosslike spots. When spawning, both sexes turn an overall bronze-purple and may acquire reddish spots on the head and body. This fish is harvested at sea during summer and early fall, while returning to spawn in the freshwater rivers and streams of its origin.

In recipes, Atlantic salmon may be used in place of trout, arctic charr or lake whitefish.

ATLANTIC SILVERSIDE (*P*)

The Atlantic silverside closely resembles its smelt and capelin relatives and is often known as sand smelt or (erroneously) capelin. These three species all have the same transparent green upper bodies, with white belly and a silver body band. The silverside grows to a length of 13.5 cm (5.5″).

Due to the perishability of its flesh, silverside is frozen whole immediately on being caught and is sold only frozen whole.

In recipes, silverside is interchangeable with smelt or capelin.

CAPELIN (P)

Closely resembling smelt, the capelin is on the average slightly larger and can reach up to 22.5 cm (9″) in length. It is transparent olive to bottle green on the upper body, with silvery sides and a white belly. Capelin ranges the high seas all year, arriving in droves to spawn on coarse sand or fine gravel beaches from Greenland to Maine in June and July.

Capelin, like smelt, is cleaned and served whole, as the bones are edible and crunchy. This makes it quick and easy to prepare. Capelin is delicious pan fried or deep fried.

In recipes, capelin may be used in place of smelt or silverside.

CUSK (G)

A relative of the cod family, cusk is also known as brismak, brosmius, tusk, torsk and moonfish. Practically unknown on the commercial market until recently, this delicious fish is gaining in popularity. Colour variations are extensive and related to its environment. Cusk can be dark red through green-brown to pale yellow. Its single dorsal fin distinguishes it from hake, which it closely resembles. Although the average length is about 60 cm (24″) and the weight usually ranges from 1 to 7 kg (2 to 15 lbs.), cusk have weighed in at 13.5 kg (30 lbs.) and measured as much as 100 cm (40″) in length. Caught mostly in the deep waters of the North Atlantic all year round, cusk is more abundant in June and July.

When cooked, cusk is very similar in taste and appearance to cod.

In recipes, cusk may be used whenever fillets are called for.

DOGFISH OR SPINY DOGFISH SHARK (G)

The dogfish is a small shark which abounds in all seas and occurs frequently in very large schools. Its main source of food is smaller fish, so dogfish may be found close to schools of herring and smelt. It is also called grayfish, spring dogfish, rock salmon and harbour halibut. Its slender, sharklike body can grow to a maximum of 123 cm (49″) and is normally slate grey on the upper body, shading to pale grey below. Dogfish has been used for food only in the last few years; its earlier use was for reduction into meal and oil. Most of the catch is exported to Europe, where dogfish fillets are used for fish and chips. As other fish species become scarce and expensive, a closer look is being taken at the dogfish to provide a cheaper alternative.

Dogfish is sold only frozen, as its flesh has a high fat content which makes it susceptible to rancidity if not handled quickly. The flesh of the dogfish also contains a small amount of urea, which causes release of ammonia as the fish ages or cooks. To counteract this problem, add 15 mL (1 Tbsp.) vinegar or 10 mL (2 tsp.) lemon juice to 1 L (1 qt.) water for each 0.5 kg (1 lb) of fish. Marinate refrigerated fillets in this solution overnight or for at least 4 hours. Handled and cooked properly, dogfish can be quite tasty.

FLOUNDER OR SOLE (G)

Many of the species of flatfish found in the North Atlantic are marketed as sole, though they actually belong to the flounder or dab families. Next to cod, these flatfish are the most important groundfish catch to the Atlantic fisheries. The principal harvest time for all flatfish species is February to October.

American plaice is the most common and commercially important flatfish. Also known as Canadian plaice, roughback, dab, sand dab or plaice, this species has a large mouth and is reddish to greyish brown on the upper body, with white to bluish white on the underside. It averages 0.9 to 1.4 kg (2 to 3 lbs.) in weight and 38 to 40 cm (15 to 16″) in length.

Yellowtail flounder may also be called rusty dab, sandy dab or mud dab. Distinctive features are its small mouth, an olive brown upper side with rusty spots, and a yellow tail. This species may reach a length of 40 cm (16″) and weigh up to 600 g (1 lb.).

Witch flounder is commonly known as gray sole or greysole, and other names are craig fluke, pale flounder, pole dab, pale dab, Torbay sole or white sole. It has a greyish brown upper side, a small mouth, and averages 45 cm (18″) in length and 700 g (1.5 lbs.) in weight.

Winter flounder may also be found under the names blackback, lemon sole or George's Bank flounder. Reddish brown to almost black, it is sometimes spotted or mottled on its eyed side. At maturity, its length is 30 cm (12″), and its average weight is 500 g (1 lb.).

Summer flounder is often known as fluke. Its compressed, oblong body is brown or grey-brown on the upper side, sometimes appearing almost black. The largest of the flounders, it reaches a maximum length of 123 cm (49"), while its average weight is 7 kg (15 lbs.).

Whether called flounder, sole, dab or plaice, fillets from this family have a delicate, lean white flesh and a delicious flavour.

In recipes, flounder may be used whenever fillets are called for. Take care not to overcook these fish, however, as their fillets are very thin.

HADDOCK (*G*)

Haddock is a popular fish on both sides of the Atlantic. A member of the cod family, haddock is generally smaller, weighing on average between 0.9 and 1.8 kg (2 to 4 lbs.) and ranging in length from 38 to 63 cm (15 to 25"). The head and back are a dark purple-grey with a black lateral line, the underside being silver-grey with a slight pink cast. These colours are distinctive of the haddock, as are the pointed first dorsal fin and a black patch between the lateral line and the middle section of the pectoral fin. Haddock may be caught all year; peak periods vary with the gear used and the area fished.

Haddock has a tasty, lean white flesh which is softer in texture than cod. Although readily available fresh on the east coast, haddock is marketed elsewhere frozen. Smoked, it is famous worldwide as finnan haddie and is also utilized in prepared convenience products and in canned chicken haddie.

In recipes, haddock may be used whenever fillets are called for.

HERRING (*P*)

This versatile, flavourful and highly nutritious fish is found in both the Pacific and Atlantic oceans. Sometimes known as digby, mattie or sea herring, the young are often referred to as sild or yawling. Herring the world over have a similar appearance, a blue-green back with silver belly, but the Atlantic species is slightly larger than its Pacific counterpart. The maximum length of an adult herring is 43 cm (17"), and its weight can vary from 250 to 750 g (0.5 to 1.5 lbs.). It normally travels in large schools and may be caught all year in the Atlantic, with the principal seasons being spring and fall.

Herring roe is composed of small yellow-orange eggs which, after a brining process, are a prized delicacy in Japan. It is quickly becoming popular in the western world as the poor man's caviar (see index).

In recipes, herring may often be used in place of mackerel.

POLLOCK OR BOSTON BLUEFISH (G)

Better known commercially under the name Boston bluefish, the Atlantic pollock also belongs to the cod family. Other common names for this fish include blisterback, merlan, merlan noire, colin, grass whiting, Margate hake, Dover hake, gallagh, greenfish, lythe, saithe and coalfish. The Atlantic pollock bears no relationship to the walleye pollock or Alaskan pollock, having a firmer flesh and a more acceptable colour and flavour. Its distinguishing features are a projecting lower jaw, pointed snout, a more rounded body and a forked rather than a square tail. It has a dark green-brown back, silver-grey sides, pale belly and white or grey lengthwise stripes. At maturity, pollock ranges from 50 to 90 cm (20 to 36″) in length and weighs from 1 to 7 kg (2 to 15 lbs.). It is caught year round, with the main catch in July and August.

In recipes, pollock may be used in place of cod, hake, haddock and most other firm-fleshed fillets.

REDFISH OR OCEAN PERCH (G)

Better known commercially as ocean perch, the redfish is of the sebastes family which is widely distributed throughout the world. It may also be known under the names rosefish, bream, Norway haddock, sea bream, berghilt, redbarsch, red perch, sebaste and soldier. Neither the redfish nor its Pacific rockfish relative is a true perch, however. This species is found in the cold deep waters along the edge of the Contintental Shelf from Baffin Island to the Gulf of Maine. The redfish, true to its name, has an orange to flame red body; it also has black eyes and a number of sharp spines on the head. A relatively small fish, it ranges in length from 20 to 40 cm (8 to 16″) and weighs from 0.5 to 1 kg (1 to 2 lbs.). The principal catch is taken in April, then June through October.

Redfish or ocean perch has a medium-firm flesh with a distinctive flavour. It is delicious baked or poached whole.

In recipes, redfish may be used whenever fillets are called for.

RED HAKE (G)

A little-known member of the cod family, this underutilized species is gaining in popularity. It is also known as squirrel hake, white hake, mud hake, ling, lingue, merluche and codling. Red hake differs from its better-known cousin, silver hake, by its slender pelvic fins and smaller number of teeth. When caught, this fish varies in weight from 1 to 5 kg (2 to 11 lbs.), and the average length ranges from 50 to 88 cm (20 to 35″). The largest weight recorded is 23 kg (50 lbs.). Caught year round, red hake is mainly harvested during the summer months.

Red hake has a white flesh which is firm and tasty.

In recipes, red hake may be used whenever fillets are called for.

SILVER HAKE (G)

This member of the cod family, also called whiting, is little known and constitutes only a moderate commercial fishery. Compared to other cods, silver hake has a longer, slimmer body, as well as a projecting lower jaw. Mature hake ranges from 23 to 35 cm (9 to 14″) in length and weighs an average of 0.7 kg (1.5 lbs.), though fish have been caught weighing up to 2.5 kg (5.5 lbs.). Its principal landing season is June through November, but it is caught year round.

Silver hake is available only frozen, as after being caught its firm flesh rapidly becomes soft. For this reason, and to obtain best results, it should be cooked from its frozen state. Fillets or whole fish are best pan fried or deep fried.

In recipes, silver hake may be used whenever fillets are called for, keeping in mind that it has a softer flesh which is apt to break up easily.

SKATE (G)

Abundant on both coasts, the skate is also known by the names skider, tinker, ginny, flanie, banjo and roker. Two Atlantic species appear predominantly on the commercial market. Resembling a large, diamond-shaped flounder with broad wings, skate is also readily distinguished by its slender, ratlike tail. It may be caught all year, but the principal fishing season is May through July.

Smooth skate is caught from Newfoundland southward. It reaches a maximum size of 62 cm (24″).

Thorny skate, also known as starry skate or Atlantic prickly skate, is by far the most abundant of the two commercially available species. It can grow to almost double the size of the smooth skate and is most often found on the Grand Banks.

Virtually unknown and untried until recently because of its unusual appearance, skate has a delicate and distinctive flavour much like that of scallops. Only the wings are cooked (see index), and the flesh is then removed with a knife or fork, giving long strips of delicious fish. It is an ideal fish for children and the elderly, since it has no bones and is easy to digest.

SWORDFISH (P)

A deep-sea species, the swordfish travels vast distances and is often found on both sides of the Atlantic. Another name for this fish is broadbill, because of its broad sword. Its smooth, nonscaly skin is another distinctive feature. The upper body is a dark, metallic purple which becomes dusky on the underside. Summer and early fall are the principal landing seasons.

Swordfish is found on the market predominantly in steak form, either fresh or frozen, and a small amount is canned.

In recipes, swordfish may be used instead of other lean, firm-fleshed fish, especially salmon, trout or halibut.

TUNA FAMILY (P)

All tunas come from the same family, but the flesh colour and flavour of the different species vary considerably. The species with the whitest flesh and most delicate flavour is the most prized and the highest priced.

Bluefin is the only tuna readily available for commercial harvesting off the Atlantic coast. Known also as tunny, horse mackerel and tuna, it is the largest of the tuna family, sometimes exceeding 454 kg (1000 lbs.). Its upper body is dark blue, while the underside shades from grey to silver-grey with spot markings. Bluefin is one of the species of tuna that, when canned, must be labelled "Light Meat." Other tuna species that come under this label are yellowfin and skipjack, which are found to a lesser extent in the Atlantic Ocean.

Albacore provides a limited catch in the south Atlantic and is one of the few tunas to be allowed the prized "White Meat" designation on the can label. The major commercial catch for the canning of albacore is by Japan in the Pacific Ocean.

Atlantic bonito must have the word "Bonito" on the can label because of its dark flesh and stronger flavour. It is metallic blue dorsally, with a silver belly and oblique parallel black lines sloping up and back. This fish reaches a length of 102 cm (41″).

In recipes, canned tuna may often be used in place of canned salmon.

TURBOT OR GREENLAND HALIBUT (G)

Turbot is pronounced with an audible "t" at the end, as is fillet. This species more closely resembles its relative the Atlantic halibut than it does the European turbot. Although it is still known by the names Greenland halibut, Greenland turbot and Newfoundland turbot, its commercial name is now simply turbot. Often called by other names such as black halibut, blue halibut, grey halibut, lesser halibut and mock halibut, it is a fish of distinction in its own right and is gaining in popularity. Turbot is greyish brown with dark pigmentation and is usually light grey on the underside. Individual fish weigh from 4.5 to 11.5 kg (10 to 25 lbs.), though some have been known to reach a weight of 50 kg (110 lbs.) and a length of 100 cm (40″). The principal landing season is from May to October.

Turbot has a higher fat content than cod or halibut and is often sold cured or smoked.

In recipes, turbot may be used whenever firm-fleshed fillets are called for.

WOLFFISH (G)

Also known as ocean catfish, Atlantic catfish, striped wolffish and ocean whitefish, wolffish should not be confused with the freshwater species of catfish or the sea catfish of the south Atlantic. Readily identified by its heavy, blennylike body, the wolffish also has a grey skin and a toothy face. Its colour varies from a slate blue to dull olive green to purplish brown, usually with ten or more dark transverse bars on the forward two-thirds of the body. Its weight varies from 1.5 to 10 kg (3 to 22 lbs.). Wolffish may be caught year round, but the principal season is in May and August.

In recipes, wolffish may be used whenever fillets are called for.

SHELLFISH

BLUE MUSSELS (*M*)

Well known for thousands of years in Great Britain and Europe, blue mussels are abundant in the Atlantic region and have become a popular item on the east coast. Mussels can be found attached to pebbles, seaweed and rocks along the waterline at low tide, but the larger specimens are taken in deeper water. Their hard shells may be blue-black, brown or brown with black rays, and they may be harvested all year in most areas. Today, the production of mussels is augmented by aquaculture.

When cooked, mussel meat turns bright orange.

In recipes, mussels are often interchangeable with other shellfish.

CLAMS (*M*)

The species of clam most harvested in the Atlantic region is commonly named the soft-shell clam or steamer. A number of other species are less abundant and less available commercially, including the hard-shell clam or quahog. Soft-shell clams grow to a maximum size of 12.5 cm (5″) and are commonly found on muddy-sandy beaches from Labrador to North Carolina. They are generally harvested from the shoreline at low tide. (Also see clams under Pacific species.)

In recipes, clams are often interchangeable with other shellfish.

LOBSTER (*CRUST*)

Often referred to as American lobster or northern lobster, this species is found in most coastal areas from the Strait of Belle Isle to the North Carolina coast. With today's technology and air transportation, lobster has become a popular delicacy worldwide. Live lobster varies considerably in colour from a dark olive green to reddish brown with shades of blue. Marketable sizes of lobster range from 0.5 to 1.5 kg (1 to 3 lbs.), though they do grow to over 5 kg (11 lbs.) and these larger lobsters are most often canned. The principal lobster season is March through July, but some fishing is carried out throughout most of the remainder of the year.

During cooking, lobster turns a characteristic bright red colour.

In recipes, lobster is often interchangeable with other shellfish.

OYSTERS (*M*)

The species of oyster most commonly found in North America is often called after the region where it is harvested, such as Blue Point, Malpeque, Cape Cod, Chincoteague, Apalachicola and Kent Island. By whatever name, these oysters are known and revered as a delicacy throughout the world. In general, they are smaller than Pacific or Japanese oysters, though they can vary in shape, growth and meat characteristics according to habitat and food supply. The shells may be flat or deep and rounded, and the colour of the meat can range from pearly to beige, and from grey to a greenish tinge. (Green in oysters is quite safe and is due to the algae on which they feed.) Most oysters for the commercial market are grown under seminatural conditions in coastal inlet "farms" from seed collected in the wild. (Also see oysters under Pacific species.)

In recipes, oysters are often interchangeable with other shellfish.

PINK SHRIMP (*CRUST*)

Often referred to as the great northern prawn or Canadian pink shrimp, this species is growing in commercial importance. (The terms "shrimp" and "prawn" are often used indiscriminately, but in commercial usage shrimp normally refers to the smaller species, and prawn to the larger.) The pink shrimp varies in size from 3 to 8 cm (1 to 3″) and is grey-green. It is usually caught in deep-water areas from Greenland to Maine, principally through spring, summer and fall.

When cooked, shrimp turns a bright pink or red.

In recipes, shrimp or prawns are often interchangeable with other shellfish.

ROCK CRAB (*CRUST*)

The commercial catch of rock crab on the Atlantic coast is small. It is not as well known or as popular as either the Dungeness or Alaska king crab, which are found off the Pacific coast. Rock crab is found mostly in coastal areas from Labrador to South Carolina. Its reddish shell has a smooth surface, and this crab is readily identifiable by its purple or crimson spots. Those sold commercially average 250 g (0.5 lb.) in weight and measure 10 cm (4″) in body width. They are caught from May through August, and most of the catch is frozen or canned. (Also see Alaska king crab and Dungeness crab under Pacific species.)

In recipes, crab is often interchangeable with other shellfish.

SEA SCALLOPS (*M*)

Commercial scallop dragging is carried out in nearshore and offshore areas of the Atlantic coast. Scallops are "shucked" or shelled as soon as they are caught and generally only the adductor muscle is taken for food. Sea scallops, also known as giant scallops and smooth scallops, are the more important of the two species that are harvested commercially. Their shell size can vary from 13 to 20.5 cm (5 to 8″), and scallops are graded by size. An average yield is approximately 80 muscles to the kilogram (36 to a pound). Sea scallops may be taken all year but their main season is March through November.

In recipes, scallops are often interchangeable with other shellfish.

SNOW CRAB (*CRUST*)

Also known as spider crab, queen crab and tanner crab, the snow crab ranges from Greenland to Maine. Its pale brown body is almost circular in outline, and its very long legs have a flattened appearance. The snow crab reaches a maximum weight of about 1.25 kg (3 lbs.) and a body width of 15 cm (6"). It is caught from June to November.

In recipes, crab may often be used in place of other shellfish.

SQUID (*M*)

This unusual-looking ocean mollusc is found off Atlantic shores from Newfoundland southward. With eight arms, two tentacles and tubular body, the squid is often ignored as a food because of prejudice due to its appearance. It reaches a maximum weight of about 700 g (1.5 lbs.) and can grow to a length of 30 to 46 cm (12 to 18"). Although squid may vary slightly in colour, it is usually white with reddish brown spots on the mantle. The principal harvest time is August through October.

Squid is a tasty food which can be cooked in a variety of ways. Consult the index for preparation techniques and recipes.

In recipes, squid may be often be used in place of octopus or abalone.

ᔥPACIFIC SPECIESᔥ
FISH

DOGFISH OR SPINY DOGFISH SHARK (*G*)

See dogfish under Atlantic species.

EULACHON/LONGFIN SMELT (*P*)

Fish in the smelt family are all relatively small, the largest being 30 cm (12″) in length, and they generally appear in large schools. Their main harvest season is late summer and early fall, when they arrive on beaches to spawn.

The eulachon closely resembles its Atlantic counterpart, the American smelt, except that it is bluish brown on the dorsal side, with a silver-white belly. It grows to a length of about 22.9 cm (9″). This fish has been used for centuries by Pacific Northwest Coast Indians as food and to produce oil for cooking. In the early days, according to some sources, the Indians fitted dried eulachon with wicks to use as candles; hence its frequently used name of candlefish.

The longfin smelt is smaller than the eulachon, reaching an average length of 15.2 cm (6″). It is pale olive brown on the dorsal side and silvery white below.

Most smelt species are rich in oil and are delicious to eat, especially deep fried or pan fried, and may be served as an appetizer or an entrée.

In recipes, eulachon and longfin smelt may be used in place of capelin or any other species of smelt.

FLOUNDER OR SOLE (G)

As in the Atlantic, there are many species (over 15) of flatfish, exclusive of halibut, to be found in Pacific waters. The species of flatfish found off the Pacific coast are similar to those in the Atlantic but have marked differences. Though commonly marketed as "sole," these fish properly belong to the flounder or dab families. (There is a Dover sole fishery on the Pacific coast but it should not be mistaken for its famous namesake, the channel or Dover sole found in European countries bordering the English Channel; the texture of the European species is considerably firmer.) Only four Pacific flounder species are of major importance to commercial fisheries here.

Brill or petrale sole is the most highly valued of the Pacific flatfish and is also the most popular. At maturity, it reaches close to 40 cm (16″) in length.

Lemon sole is so named because of its delicate lemon flavour, not because it bears any resemblance to the true lemon sole of Europe. It is also known as English, common or California sole. Lemon sole has a narrow pointed head, a uniform light brown colouring on the eyed side and a white to creamy white belly. Fish of commercial size range from 35 to 39 cm (14″ to 16″) in length.

Rock sole is commonly called roughback because of its rough scaly skin. Its colour is variable, mostly browns and greys, with a white to yellowish belly. It is similar in size to the lemon sole.

Turbot or arrowtooth flounder should not be mistaken for the more famous Atlantic turbot (see turbot under Atlantic species). It is distinguishable from other flatfish by its large teeth and can grow to a length of 90 cm (36″). An inexpensive and tasty fish, its fillets have juicy large flakes, rather like cod. Until a few years ago, it was relatively unused for food but is fast becoming popular as an alternative to cod and sole.

In recipes, fish from this family, whether called flounder or sole, may be used whenever fillets are called for. Keep in mind, however, that fillets from these species are thin and care must be taken not to overcook them.

GREY OR PACIFIC COD (G)

This is the true cod of the Pacific and closely resembles the more famous cod of the North Atlantic. The Pacific cod is brown to grey on the back, lighter on the sides, with the belly shading to white. At maturity, it reaches an average size of 40 cm (16″) and a weight of 3 to 4 kg (6 to 9 lbs.), though some have been known to measure over 100 cm (40″) in length. One of the most important commercial species caught in the Pacific, it is landed year round, with the largest catches being made in the winter months.

When cooked, this cod has fairly large flakes of white succulent meat and is equally delicious baked, broiled, pan fried or poached.

In recipes, grey or Pacific cod may be used in place of most other white-fleshed fish.

LINGCOD (*G*)

Not related to either the grey cod or sablefish (Alaska black cod), lingcod is one of the larger of the commercially caught fishes in Pacific waters. Other names for this fish include blue cod, buffalo cod, green cod, greenling, leopard cod and cultus cod. It has a slender body, mottled dark grey and brown, a large mouth and prominent teeth. Some reach a weight of 25 to 30 kg (55 to 66 lbs.), but the average fish weighs 5 to 6 kg (11 to 13 lbs.). It is caught year round.

The raw flesh of the lingcod is sometimes slightly greenish in colour but, when cooked, it turns white and has a fine, delicate flavour.

In recipes, lingcod may be used in place of any white-fleshed fish.

PACIFIC HAKE (*G*)

Also known as Pacific whiting, Pacific hake is closely related to grey or Pacific cod and to walleye pollock. It is also related to many other species of hake found on the continental shelves of Europe, Africa, North and South America and New Zealand. Its grounds range from the Gulf of Alaska to the Gulf of California. The average Pacific hake is 50 cm (20″) in length and weighs about 1 kg (2 lbs.).

Pacific hake has softer flesh than many of its cod relatives and requires immediate chilling to prevent deterioration. However, when properly processed, it has a mild flavour and delicate texture. It is becoming increasingly popular as a tasty and inexpensive alternative to some species which are better known. Because of its characteristically soft flesh, this fish is best cooked from its frozen state and either pan fried or deep fried.

In recipes, Pacific hake may be used in place of sole or whenever flaked fish is called for.

PACIFIC HALIBUT (G)

Similar and closely related to the Atlantic species, the Pacific halibut ranges from the Bering Sea to California. Halibut used to be one of the most important commercial fish in the Pacific, but due to overfishing and mismanagement the allowable catch has been drastically reduced in order to conserve the fishery. Fifteen to twenty years ago, it was common to catch halibut weighing from 100 to 200 kg (220 to 440 lbs.), but today fish are rarely caught over 20 kg (44 lbs.). Very strict regulations are applied by the International Pacific Halibut Commission on the size and quantity of fish caught.

When cooked, the flesh of halibut tends to be dry, but it can be a king among fishes if handled and cooked properly. Although sold fresh to restaurants and retail markets, it often appears in stores frozen in steak form. (Also see Atlantic halibut.)

In recipes, Pacific halibut may often be substituted for salmon and may be used whenever firm-fleshed fish is called for.

PACIFIC HERRING (P)

This close relative of the Atlantic herring mainly ranges and feeds on the banks and edges of the continental shelf of the North Pacific, coming close to shore only during the spawning season. Herring belongs to the same family as pilchard and shad and like them travels in large schools. In addition to being of great commercial importance, herring is of incalculable value indirectly as a food supply for other fish such as coho and chinook salmon, cod and lingcod. Herring is sold both domestically and abroad and is much in demand; without strict management regarding limits and quotas caught, it is in danger of being overfished. (Also see herring under Atlantic species.)

Delicious when cooked, herring and pilchard are very inexpensive and easy to prepare. Herring roe eggs are small; when brined they become amber in colour and are considered a great delicacy. The spring herring roe harvest is sold almost exclusively to Japan.

In recipes, Pacific herring is generally interchangeable with mackerel, shad and pilchard.

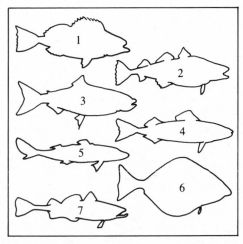

Pacific Fish

1. Pacific Ocean perch
2. Grey cod or Pacific cod
3. Chinook salmon
4. Sablefish or Alaska black cod
5. Dogfish or spiny dogfish shark
6. Pacific halibut
7. Pacific hake

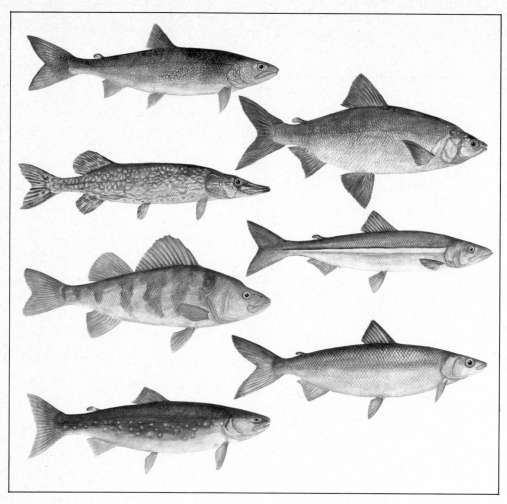

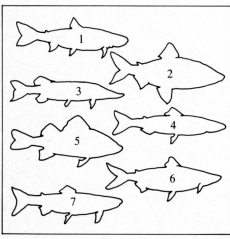

FRESHWATER FISH

1. Lake trout
2. Lake whitefish
3. Northern pike
4. Rainbow smelt
5. Yellow perch
6. Tullibee or cisco or lake herring
7. Arctic charr

ROCKFISH:
PACIFIC OCEAN PERCH/PACIFIC RED SNAPPER (G)

Rockfish constitute a group of many species which are predominant in the northern temperate seas. Frequently misnamed "rockcods," they have no close relationship to the true cods. Well over 50 species of rockfish are known along the eastern shores of the Pacific Ocean. Most are readily identifiable by their wide mouths, spiny dorsal fin and brilliant colours which vary from reds and oranges to browns and greens, though only Pacific red snapper, canary (or orange) rockfish, Pacific Ocean perch and some deep-sea species are red or orange. Rockfish can also be black with a yellow stripe, white with vertical red bars, pink with horizontal green stripes and yellow-brown. Rockfish may be harvested year round.

Many rockfish species have gained popularity and are known and marketed by their individual names, such as Pacific red snapper and Pacific Ocean perch (also called longjaw rockfish). Not a true perch, this fish is bright red with olive stippling on the side. It has a projecting lower jaw and often reaches a length of up to 50 cm (20″) and a weight of 0.75 to 1.5 kg (1.5 to 3 lbs.). (Also see redfish or ocean perch under Atlantic species.)

All rockfish have medium-firm white flesh and are delicious baked or poached whole.

In recipes, rockfish may be used whenever white-fleshed fish fillets are called for.

SABLEFISH OR ALASKA BLACK COD (G)

Better known as Alaska black cod, but misnamed because it is not a true cod, sablefish is considered one of the best of the smoked fishes. Other names for sablefish include blue cod, bluefish, Pacific black cod, candlefish, coal cod and coalfish. A medium-sized, streamlined fish, the sablefish has a black or grey-black upper body with a light grey belly. The average size harvested is 55 to 85 cm (22 to 34″) in length, with a weight of 2 to 3 kg (4.5 to 6.5 lbs.). The largest ones caught have measured over 90 cm (36″) and weighed up to 20 kg (44 lbs.)

Sablefish is rarely sold fresh on the market here because of the high oil content of its flesh. However, it is enjoyed fresh in Japan and with proper handling and marketing may become popular as a fresh product here in the near future. When smoked, the surface of the flesh takes on a yellowish colour and, after cooking, it has large flakes of juicy white meat and a delicious, distinctive smoked flavour.

In recipes, smoked sablefish may be used in place of other smoked fish.

SALMON FAMILY (A)

Five different species of salmon, differing significantly in size, colour, and migratory and spawning patterns, are harvested from the Pacific Ocean. Their flesh may be white, pink or red, but the nutritional value of all species is similar, varying only in fat content. The time of year also determines the level of fat in salmon.

Sockeye, also known as red salmon or blueback, is the most valuable of all Pacific salmon because of its uniformity of size, bright red flesh and high oil content. It is used primarily for canning, since it retains its red colour after cooking. At maturity, its weight is between 2.5 and 3.5 kg (5.5 to 8 lbs.), and its length is about 85 cm (34″). This fish has a relatively short but colourful life. The main harvest takes place during the summer and early fall, when it returns from the Pacific to spawn in the river beds or lakes where it hatched, swimming as far as 1600 km (1000 miles) upstream. At the beginning of its long journey, the spawning sockeye starts to change colour. From silver, shading to greenish blue on the back (which also shows fine black specks), its body gradually becomes bright crimson, with a green head. The male also develops a pronounced hump on the back and a sharp, hooked nose. When spawning is over, the life cycle of the sockeye is finished, and it dies within a short time.

Coho, or cohoe, is silver on the sides and metallic blue on the back, and from this gets its other names such as blueback, silver salmon and silversides. This fish weighs from 3 to 6 kg (6.5 to 13 lbs.) at maturity. The adult coho migrates upstream in early fall to spawn. Unlike sockeye, it spawns in rivers close to the ocean, though some have been known to travel as far as 640 km (400 miles) inland. Coho is harvested from mid-June to November and is also one of the most popular of game fish for sports fishermen. The bulk of the catch is marketed fresh or frozen, but some is canned and is valued next to sockeye.

Pink salmon is nicknamed humpback or humpy because of the grotesque humped back the male develops on the spawning grounds. In a very short life of two years, it reaches a remarkable 1.5 to 3 kg (3 to 6.5 lbs.), with a few weighing as much as 5 kg (11 lbs.). When spawning, this species of salmon changes colour from bright silver to a bluish grey on the back, with sides shaded red or yellow on the males and olive green on the females. This salmon contrasts markedly with the bright red and green of spawning sockeye and is less easily seen, since its colours merge in with the natural environment. The principal landing season is from July to September. Commercially, pink salmon is used chiefly for canning, and the colour of the canned fish is a delicate pink.

Chum, also known as keta, dog, qualla, calico or fall salmon, weighs from 4 to 9 kg (9 to 20 lbs.) at maturity, though weights of up to 16 kg (35 lbs.) have been recorded. It is the last of the Pacific salmon to spawn and starts its upstream migration in late fall. In the advanced stages of spawning, it changes colour to black or grey or reddish brown, and the male develops a grotesque hooked nose that exposes its sharp doglike teeth. Chum is harvested mainly from July to November and may be canned, dry-salted or frozen. Its flesh is a paler pink than that of pink salmon.

Chinook is also known as spring, tyee, king or quinnat salmon. It is a very popular sports fish and is easily identified by the black spotting on a blue-green back. It is the largest of the salmon family, with weight at maturity ranging from 5 to 25 kg (11 to 55 lbs.), though weights as high as 63 kg (140 lbs.) have been recorded. Its migration pattern differs considerably from other species of salmon; it favours spring and fall but may be seen going upriver almost any time of year. Those migrating in the earlier months tend to travel the farthest, sometimes as far as 1600 km (1000 miles) inland, while those migrating later in the year may travel only a short distance to their spawning grounds. Unlike sockeye or coho, chinook undergoes only a minor colour change during spawning, turning a dull dark brown. The harvest takes place mainly from April to October, and chinook is sold on the market fresh or frozen. The flesh varies from a bright red through various shades of pink to white.

In recipes, salmon may be used in place of arctic charr, trout or other firm-fleshed fish. Canned salmon may often be substituted for canned tuna.

SKATE *(G)*

Skate is an unusual looking fish, resembling a diamond-shaped sole. The skates are represented by many species; the best known commercially is the big skate, which has been known to reach 180 cm (72″) in length and to weigh up to 100 kg (220 lbs.). (Also see skate under Atlantic species.)

Skate wings look quite different from other fish fillets but are easy to prepare with the right knowledge. For preparation techniques and recipes, see the index.

STEELHEAD TROUT (A)

A member of the salmon family, steelhead trout more closely resembles Atlantic salmon than any of the Pacific species. Like Atlantic salmon, it may spawn more than once and return to the sea after each spawning. The young steelhead spends two to three years in fresh water before migrating out to sea; some remain in fresh water all their lives and are known as rainbow trout. The steelhead is metallic blue on the dorsal surface, silvery on the sides, with black spots on the back, dorsal and caudal fins. Although many species of trout are highly prized as splendid sports fish, the steelhead is the only one with any value on the commercial market. Other trout found in rivers and in the waters off the Pacific coast are brown, coastal cutthroat and brook trout, as well as Dolly Varden.

In recipes, trout may often be used in place of salmon.

WALLEYE POLLOCK OR ALASKAN POLLOCK (G)

More walleye pollock is landed by all nations than any other species of fish. It should not be confused with Atlantic pollock (Boston bluefish), which is a different species. On our Pacific coast, walleye pollock is one of the lesser known species, though growing in popularity. Also known as bigeye pollock because of its extra large eyes, walleye pollock is readily identifiable by its projecting lower jaw and slim body. It is olive green to brown on the back, with silvery sides. This fish grows to an average of 45 to 55 cm (18 to 22″) in length at maturity and may be caught year round.

Walleye pollock has a softer flesh than cod but when handled properly is delicious. Pollock roe is a growing fishery, with most of the product being sold to the Japanese market.

In recipes, walleye pollock may often be used when fillets are called for.

SHELLFISH

Alaska King Crab (*CRUST*)

Alaska king crab occurs mainly off the Queen Charlotte Islands and along the coastline of Alaska. Averaging up to 100 cm (40″) from tip to tip, it has a small body with a hard shell, and long legs with one large and one small claw. A premium gourmet food, many people prefer its prized leg meat over that of lobster or other crabmeat. It is normally harvested from August through November, and fishing is prohibited during the breeding season in February and March.

In recipes, crab may often be used in place of other shellfish.

Blue Mussels (*M*)

See blue mussels under Atlantic species.

Clams (*M*)

On the Pacific coast there are many species of clams, but only five are used commercially to any extent. (Also see clams under Atlantic species.)

The butter clam is the most abundant commercial species and is used extensively for canning and for making chowders. The shell is oval and the average size of those in the commercial catch is about 7.5 cm (3″) in length.

The little-neck clam is also known as the Pacific little-neck, rock cockle or native little-neck. It is smaller than the butter clam, and the average market size is about 5 cm (2″) in length. It is usually marketed fresh or frozen and is used as a steamer clam.

The Japanese or Manila little-neck clam was accidentally introduced to the Pacific coast when oyster seeds were imported from Japan. It closely resembles the little-neck clam but is more oblong in shape, darker in colour and may be mottled with brown or black. Also, it can be readily distinguished from the little-neck clam because the tip of its siphon is split for about 5 mm (0.25″). The average size of Japanese clams in the commercial market is about 5 cm (2″). Like the little-neck clam, it is usually marketed fresh or frozen for the steamer clam trade.

The razor clam occurs only on surf-swept sandy beaches. The average commercial size is about 15 cm (6″). It may be eaten fried or in chowders and has an excellent flavour.

The geoduck clam (pronounced goo-ee-duck) is the largest clam in North America and may measure up to 23 cm (9″) and weigh up to 4 kg (9 lbs.). Harvest is entirely by divers. The meat may be steaked and fried, or canned and used in chowders.

The horse clam is also known as the gaper, empire or otter shell clam. Measuring up to 20 cm (8″) in length, it almost equals the large size of the geoduck clam. It is distinguished from the geoduck by tentacles on the inner edge. The horse clam is harvested year round. The siphon and body meat are frozen and sold separately.

In recipes, clams may often be used in place of other shellfish.

DUNGENESS CRAB (*CRUST*)

Sometimes called market crab, Dungeness is the best-known species of crab on the Pacific coast. It is bluish-brown on the back and a light sand colour underneath. At maturity, it can reach a maximum width of 25 cm (10″) and weigh from 0.8 to 1.8 kg (1.75 to 4 lbs.). Strict regulations govern the commercial and sports fishery for this crab. The shell must measure not less than 16.5 cm (6.5″) across the broadest part. The Dungeness crab, usually located on sandy ground in shallow water, is becoming increasingly hard to find. Fishing is done year round using crab traps.

In recipes, crab may often be used in place of other shellfish.

NORTHERN ABALONE (*M*)

The fishery for abalone is concentrated in the northern coastal region, where the northern abalone prefers sheltered waters. Often called pink or pinto abalone, earshell and venus' ear, this species has a wavy pink outer shell, the inner surface of which is an attractive iridescent mother-of-pearl. It may be harvested year round. For preparation techniques and recipes, see the index.

OCTOPUS (M)

Although the giant Pacific octopus deserves recognition as an interesting and useful sea creature, it has earned an undeserved reputation as a monster from the deep. It grows rapidly and may reach weights greater than 45.5 kg (100 lbs.) within the space of five years, and individuals have been recorded at over 182 kg (400 lbs.). However, most of those caught commercially weigh less than 32 kg (70 lbs.), with a stretched length of about 4.5 m (15'). Interest in the commercial fishing of octopus has increased recently, for use as halibut bait and for the expanding export food markets. It may be caught year round.

In recipes, octopus may be used in place of squid or abalone.

PACIFIC OYSTERS (M)

Many species of oysters occur in Pacific waters, but only the Pacific oyster is marketed commercially. The original stock of these oysters was imported from Japan in about 1912. Most of those marketed are grown on oyster farms and have an average length of 12 to 18 cm (5 to 7").

Contrary to popular belief, oysters are not poisonous in months without the letter ''r,'' but the meat is soft or watery during the reproductive period and is of less commercial value at that time. Most oysters are marketed fresh or frozen in a shucked state: that is, the meat has been removed from the shell. (Also see oysters under Atlantic species.)

In recipes, oysters may often be used in place of other shellfish.

SHRIMP (CRUST)

Of the many species of shrimp found off the Pacific coast, only a few are harvested for the commercial market.

These include sidestripe or giant red shrimp; pink shrimp; prawn or spot shrimp; humpback or king shrimp; and coonstripe shrimp. From tiny shrimp to good-sized prawns, they vary in size from 5 to 20 cm (2 to 8″) and are harvested year round.

Shrimp and prawns, like all crustaceans, change colour from grey-green to bright pink or red when cooked.

In recipes, shrimp or prawns may often be used in place of other shellfish.

SQUID (*M*)

See squid under Atlantic species.

෨FRESHWATER SPECIES෨

ARCTIC CHARR

Arctic charr is a delicacy and in North America can be found in Alaska and northern Canada. With an elongated body somewhat typical of salmon and trout, arctic charr is silvery, with a deep blue or greenish blue back and upper sides. Sometimes small pink spots are noticeable along and below the lateral line. When spawning, this fish turns a brilliant red or orange, varying according to the region. Harvesting is carried on year round, but the species cannot withstand heavy exploitation and the commercial fishery is carefully managed.

There are two distinct types of arctic charr.

Anadromous or sea-run arctic charr migrates to the sea in the summer to feed, returning to fresh water for the winter. Its average size is from 1 to 5 kg (2 to 11 lbs.), though some caught have weighed 14 kg (31 lbs.).

Landlocked arctic charr remains in fresh water for its entire life. This type matures earlier and reaches an average weight of only 1 to 2 kg (2 to 4 lbs.).

The colour of the flesh, like that of chinook salmon, may vary from an orange-red to pink or even white.

In recipes, arctic charr may be used in place of salmon, trout or other firm-fleshed fish.

CARP

Also known as German, European, mirror and leather carp, this fish is not as yet widely known or accepted in North America as it is in Europe and Asia. However, small gains in popularity are being achieved by some entrepreneurs who are marketing small- and medium-sized carp alive out of tanks. The carp's colour is usually olive green on the back, becoming yellowish on the belly. The average commercially caught fish frequently exceeds 7 kg (15 lbs.) in weight, and some have been recorded over 23 kg (50.5 lbs.).

In recipes, fresh carp may be used in place of cod, haddock and pollock (Boston bluefish); smoked carp may be used instead of any other smoked fish.

GOLDEYE

This fish is more popularly known in its smoked state as Winnipeg goldeye, which is a prized delicacy. Goldeye closely resembles herring in colour, being dark blue to blue-green on the back and upper sides, with the ventral surface shading to white. Weight may vary considerably, depending on the region in which the fish is caught, but in general goldeye weighs an average of 0.5 to 1 kg (1 to 2 lbs.) and measures 25 to 30 cm (10 to 12″) in length.

Goldeye is rarely sold fresh on the market, as in its fresh form it is both insipid of flavour and unappetizing of colour. The popular smoked goldeye is bright red through orange to golden, a colour once achieved through smoking with willow wood but now largely produced by harmless food dyes.

In recipes, smoked goldeye may be used in place of any other smoked fish.

INCONNU

This fish received its name from early French settlers, who called it "poisson inconnu" or unknown fish because it was the first of its kind they had ever seen. Anglers often refer to it as connie, coney or sheefish. Inconnu is silvery overall, usually green to light brown on the back, with the dorsal fin dusky at the tip. Although it is not uncommon to catch fish weighing up to 15 kg (33 lbs.), the average one taken is 4 to 6 kg (9 to 13 lbs.).

The flesh of inconnu is white and tender.

In recipes, inconnu may be substituted for salmon, trout or other firm-fleshed fish.

LAKE TROUT

Lake trout belongs to the salmon family and is the largest of the trouts. It is also known by other names such as great lake trout, grey trout, salmon trout, Great Lakes charr, mackinaw, togue and touladi. Its body colour may vary from almost black to very light green. The largest lake trout caught in North America weighed 46 kg (102 lbs.), though the average fish caught commercially is 2.5 to 5 kg (5.5 to 11 lbs.). This fish may be caught all year.

Lake trout is a very popular fish with firm, delicious flesh that ranges in colour from pale ivory through to a deep pink.

In recipes, lake trout may be used in place of salmon.

LAKE WHITEFISH

Whitefish is king in freshwater country. A member of the salmon and trout family, it is a valuable commercial fish in both North America and Europe. The average whitefish weighs about 1.5 kg (3 lbs.) and measures close to 45 cm (18″) in length, though it may be found considerably larger. The overall colouration is silvery, the back greenish brown to dark brown, with silvery sides and silvery white belly. The tail fin is deeply forked, and the head and mouth are comparatively small for its size. Whitefish is caught year round.

The flesh of this fish is white and, when cooked, has large juicy flakes. It has a delicate, somewhat sweet flavour.

In recipes, lake whitefish may be used in place of salmon, trout, halibut or other firm-fleshed fish.

MULLET

The mullet is only one of about sixteen species of the sucker family to be harvested commercially. It reaches an average weight of 500 g (1 lb.) and may attain a maximum weight of 3.5 kg (8 lbs.) and a length of 35 cm (14″). Mullet is caught principally in the spring, on its way to spawn in the fast-flowing rivers that feed the large lakes of its normal habitat.

The flesh of the mullet is white and soft textured.

In recipes, mullet should be used when flaked fish is called for, because of its soft flesh.

NORTHERN PIKE

Northern pike is found in lakes and quiet rivers in most of freshwater country. It is popular as a sports fish and also appears on the commercial market in many forms. Sometimes referred to as jackfish, it has a dark green, elongated body, mottled with lighter spots, and a yellow-white underside. Its large mouth bristles with sharp, pointed teeth. The average weight varies from 1 to 2 kg (2 to 4 lbs.), though some have been taken weighing as much as 20 kg (44 lbs.).

When cooked, the flesh of pike is white, firm and flaky.

In recipes, pike may be used whenever firm-fleshed fillets, steaks or whole fish are called for.

PICKEREL OR WALLEYE

Known by many other names such as yellow pickerel, walleye pike, yellow pike—and doré in Quebec because of its golden appearance—the succulent pickerel is generally thought to be one of the best eating fish anywhere. Pickerel colouration is highly variable, depending on its habitat. Background colours range from olive brown to yellow (back darker, sides paler), with brassy mottling on the sides and yellow-white on the belly. The average weight of commercially caught fish is 1 to 2 kg (2 to 4 lbs.), but some have been known to reach 10 kg (22 lbs.). Important as both a sports and a commercial fish, pickerel is caught throughout the year.

Pickerel has a firm, flaky white flesh and fine flavour.

In recipes, pickerel may be used whenever firm-fleshed fish is called for.

RAINBOW SMELT

Rainbow smelt, sometimes known as American smelt on the Atlantic coast, is landlocked in the Great Lakes system. It has a transparent olive to bottle green back, with paler sides and a silvery belly. This fish is the basis of a large commercial catch and is harvested year round, though the main season is April and May. (See American smelt under Atlantic species.)

In recipes, the sweet-tasting rainbow smelt may be used in place of smelt or capelin.

RAINBOW TROUT

Well known to anglers, this member of the salmon family is somewhat smaller than its close relative, the steelhead trout. Rainbow trout differs from steelhead by its readily distinguishable pink to red band along the body sides and a large number of small black dots, mostly above the lateral line. Its colours vary considerably according to region and habitat. It reaches an average length of 30 to 45 cm (12 to 18″) and rarely weighs over 8 kg (18 lbs.). Pond-reared fish from Europe and Japan, weighing about 500 to 750 g (1 to 1.5 lbs.), have become very popular because they provide a uniform portion size.

The flesh of rainbow trout varies from a rich red through shades of pink to white. It is delicious baked, broiled, barbecued or poached.

In recipes, rainbow trout may be used in place of salmon.

SAUGER

A relative of the pickerel, sauger is also known as yellow walleye, sand pike or sand pickerel. It is a small fish, rarely exceeding 45 cm (18″) in length or 500 g (1 lb.) in weight. The background colour of sauger is sandy to brown; its dorsal surface is brown, with paler sides and white on the underside. One way to distinguish it from pickerel is the presence of scales on its cheeks. This fish is harvested throughout the year.

Regardless of its small size, sauger is a popular and tasty fish.

In recipes, sauger may be used whenever lean fish, fillets or whole, is called for.

TULLIBEE OR CISCO OR LAKE HERRING

The collective term "tullibee" was used by the early fur traders to cover a group of more than fourteen species of cisco or lake herring found in western freshwater lakes. These species include deepwater, longjaw, shortjaw, shortnose and blackfin cisco. Tullibee are also known as chub, though chub is also used to describe small carp. The overall colouration of tullibee is silvery; the back varies from black to blue to green to tan, with the sides silvery and the belly white. The form and size of the body differs according to the species, with the larger being about 35 cm (14″) in length and weighing about 1 kg (2 lbs.). In some parts of freshwater country, however, tullibee have been weighed in at 3.5 kg (8 lbs.). They may be caught throughout the year.

Tullibee are excellent pan fried, as are most small fish. They are often sold smoked as well as fresh.

In recipes, smoked tullibee may be used in place of any other smoked fish.

YELLOW PERCH

Yellow perch is found in lakes, ponds and quiet streams throughout freshwater territory as far north as Great Slave Lake. It is yellowish overall, with vertical bars of darker colour. A small fish, it averages 22 cm (9″) in length and 250 g (0.5 lb.) in weight. Important as both a commercial and sports fish, it may be caught all year round.

This fish is lean and sweet-tasting and is excellent broiled or pan fried.

2

CONSUMER GUIDE

AVAILABILITY

BUYING RULES—
WHAT TO LOOK FOR

PREPARATION TECHNIQUES

STORING FISH AND SHELLFISH
IN THE HOME

NUTRITION

ᖷAVAILABILITYᖷ

Both roundfish and flatfish are sold whole or in a variety of cuts. Fish and shellfish are also available in many forms: fresh, frozen, smoked, dried, salted, canned and pickled.

CUTS OF ROUNDFISH

Roundfish include all the salmon family, trout, cod, lingcod, haddock, pollock or Boston bluefish, hake, cusk, wolffish, rockfish, redfish or ocean perch, herring, shad, alewife, smelt, capelin, dogfish, swordfish, mackerel and tuna. These are available whole or in the various cuts shown here.

Whole fish are marketed just as they are when they are taken from the water. Before cooking, entrails, gills, fins and scales should be removed. The head and tail may be left on if desired. Very small roundfish like smelt and trout are frequently cooked with only the entrails removed. When purchasing whole fish, allow one serving per 500 g (1 lb.).

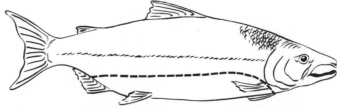

Dressed fish, sometimes called drawn or gutted, are sold with entrails and gills removed. To prepare for cooking, fins and scales should be removed. The head and tail may be left on. Allow one serving per 500 g (1 lb.).

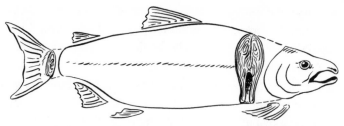

Pan-dressed fish have had the head, tail, fins, gills, entrails and scales removed. They are ready to cook as purchased. Very large fish are often cut into 0.5 to 1 kg (1 to 2 lb.) pieces. Allow two servings per 500 g (1 lb.).

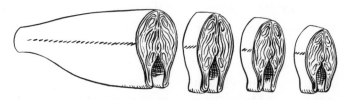

Steaks are cross-section slices of large roundfish and are ready to cook. Very large steaks may be divided by cutting through the backbone. Steaks are usually 1.25 to 2.5 cm (0.5 to 1″) thick. Allow two to three servings per 500 g (1 lb.).

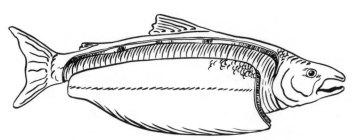

Fillets are sides of fish cut lengthwise from the backbone and are ready to cook. They should be practically boneless and very often the skin has been removed as well. A fillet from one side of a fish is a single fillet. Two sides of a small fish, with backbone removed but still joined by uncut skin, form a butterfly fillet. Allow three servings per 500 g (1 lb.).

CUTS OF FLATFISH

Flatfish include all fish from the sole, flounder or dab families, halibut and turbot. They are sold whole and in some of the same cuts shown for roundfish.

Whole flatfish may be sold just as they are when caught, if they are small. Before cooking, the head, tail, entrails, gills and fins should be removed. Flatfish cooked whole are easier to bone; fillets may be simply eased off the backbone. Allow one serving per 500 g (1 lb.).

Flatfish are most often sold in fillet form, usually skinned as well, unless the fillets are very thin (such as small sole). If unskinned, a fish will have one fillet with dark skin and one with light. Both are safe to eat, though many people prefer to remove the dark skin before cooking. Fillets from flatfish are more likely to be completely free of bones than those from roundfish. Allow two to three servings per 500 g (1 lb.).

Halibut and turbot are the only flatfish large enough to provide steaks, which are usually sold frozen. Often the cross-section is so large that the steaks have to be cut into serving-size portions. Allow two to three servings per 500 g (1 lb.).

Skate is a unique species of flatfish. It is usually prepared for sale by cutting off the wings in wide strips right through the cartilage. The wings are sometimes available fresh but most often are frozen. Allow one serving per 500 g (1 lb.).

Fresh and Frozen Fish

The seasonal habits of many fish, combined with a number of problems pertinent to the fishing industry (such as weather), make it impossible to provide fresh fish at all times, though certain species may be available year round. The seasons of specific species of fish are given elsewhere in this book. The development of quick freezing and the wide use of freezer storage and refrigerated transport vehicles, however, has made it possible to provide fish in a frozen state at any time of the year. When carefully handled through the distribution system and in the home, frozen fish retains its freshness and may be used interchangeably with fresh fish.

Small dressed fish are available frozen, as are pieces of larger fish and steaks. Frozen fish is commonly sold in the form of fillets in 500 g (1 lb.) cartons. Individually quick frozen (IQF) fillets are sold in cartons of various weights. Packages of fillets are boxed and wrapped for easy handling in supermarkets and grocery stores, though in this form the consumer is not able to judge the appearance of the fish. Also available on the market are many prepared and ready-to-cook packs of frozen fish: fish sticks (breaded or battered), fish cakes, fish portions (breaded or plain, with or without sauce) and specialty shellfish dishes.

SMOKED, DRIED AND SALTED FISH

Smoked fish include such species as Atlantic cod, sablefish (Alaska black cod), goldeye, tullibee, haddock, salmon, herring, eel and lake whitefish. The smoking treatment produces a distinctive flavour but does not preserve the fish, which must be handled and stored with as much care as fresh fish. Kippered herrings are sold both salt-cured and smoked. Dried salt cod may be purchased either shredded or as boneless fillets, usually packaged in 500 g (1 lb.) wooden boxes.

CANNED FISH

Fish are most widely distributed in the canned form. From the standpoint of total annual production and quantity consumption, the most important of the fish canned is Pacific salmon in all its many species: sockeye, coho, chinook, pink and chum.

Canned tuna is a close second in popularity. There are significant differences in the colour, flavour and price of the different species of tuna which are canned. Albacore is one of the only tunas to be allowed the prized "White Meat" label on the can because of its white flesh and delicate flavour; it is used most often for salads and sandwiches. Bluefin, yellowfin and skipjack are labelled "Light Meat" and are darker in colour and stronger in flavour than albacore; they provide practically the same nutrition and are a perfect substitute for any dish such as loaves, casseroles, and crepe or omelette fillings which do not require the perfection of albacore.

Other canned fish products are mackerel, sardines, herring, chicken haddie, kippered snacks, pickled and smoked pastes, chowders, fish cakes and creamed fish.

FISH ROE

Roe is the egg sac of the female just before spawning. The size and colour (white to deep orange) of the eggs vary, depending on the species. Roe has been a popular delicacy in Japan for centuries and is also a favourite food in northern Europe. It is becoming better known and accepted on the domestic market as consumers become more familiar with its preparation and taste. The increasing popularity of roe from many species of fish occurs at a time when the world's supply of sturgeon caviar, chiefly from Iran and the USSR, is diminishing. North American fish which yield edible roe for domestic and world markets include the salmon and trout families, herring, walleye pollock, shad, mackerel, cod, haddock, tuna, lake whitefish and northern pike.

Sturgeon roe provides the authentic, most expensive caviar on the market. The eggs are medium size, black, and very salty after curing. Salmon and whitefish roe are similarly processed and artificially coloured black to provide a less expensive version of "caviar."

For instructions on the preparation of caviar and for recipes using fish roe, see the index.

Fresh, Frozen and Canned Shellfish

Crustaceans caught off the Atlantic and Pacific coasts include crab, lobster, shrimp and prawns. Molluscs harvested off both coasts are oysters, clams, mussels, scallops and squid.

Crab is sold in different forms, depending on the species. Dungeness crab is sold live, cooked or frozen whole. Alaska king crab legs and claws are available frozen. Shelled meat from both these species of Pacific crab is also marketed fresh, frozen or sometimes canned. Snow crab legs and claws are sold frozen. Rock crab and snow crab meat are available frozen, canned or incorporated into convenience products.

Lobster is marketed live, cooked whole or frozen cooked. Lobster meat may be sold either frozen in cans or cooked and sealed under pressure in cans. This canned frozen lobster meat must be kept frozen until use, since it has not been sterilized by heat processing. Secondary prepared products such as paste and lobster cocktail are also made using lobster meat.

Shrimp and prawns are marketed in the shell, head on or headless, fresh or frozen. Frozen raw shrimp are known as "green shrimp." They are also sold as shelled cooked meat. Most Pacific shrimp are of a small pink variety. The pink shrimp caught off the Atlantic coast is somewhat larger and is often called a prawn.

Oysters are occasionally available in the shell, live or frozen, particularly the famous east coast Malpeque. However, oysters are most commonly sold as shucked meat, fresh or frozen. Prebreaded, frozen oysters are popular with the restaurant trade. Some oysters are canned, some are smoked and canned, and frozen or canned oyster stew may be found in supermarkets.

Clams are sold live in the shell and as shucked meat in fresh, frozen or canned forms. Clam chowder is also available frozen or canned.

Blue mussels are more readily available on the east coast, where they are sold fresh, shell on or shucked. Some are canned.

Sea scallops are sold fresh or frozen. The round, marshmallow-shaped muscles are graded by size before being marketed. Scallops are also used in convenience foods.

Squid may be found whole, either fresh or frozen. Frozen squid tubes, tentacles and hoods (sometimes skinless) are also available.

Abalone is available fresh or frozen in the shell, as frozen steaks, or canned.

DULSE *(SEAWEED)*

Dulse is a species of seaweed similar to the Japanese dried seaweed product called "nori." Dulse is hand picked during low tide and taken to impoundment tanks where it is rolled in seawater to expose it to the sun. The sunlight and the cleansing action of the constantly renewed seawater fill the fragile fronds with extra colour and nutrients. (The plant not only remains fully alive in the tanks but if left for a time will become encircled by the tiny, heart-shaped tips of new sprouts.) When it is glowing with tiny luminescent blue balls, the dulse is gently removed from the tank and taken to the sun-heated rocks of a drying field.

Dulse is a nourishing and highly digestible food. About 100 g (3.5 oz.) per day will provide a person's daily protein needs. It is rich in minerals, primarily potassium and calcium, but is also a significant source of iron, sodium, iodine and other trace elements. It is also a good source of vitamins, including B1, B12, C, D and E.

Before serving, dulse may be washed if desired, but washing leaches out many of the 20 amino acids present and reduces the natural salts. It should be inspected, like other leafy greens, to be sure it is free from anything undesirable such as small stones or bits of shell.

Use dulse in salads, chowders, stews, soups and casseroles to enhance their flavour and increase their nutritional value. It may be toasted and crushed to decorate hors d'oeuvre or open-faced sandwiches; it may also be used to make herb tea.

BUYING RULES—WHAT ✍TO LOOK FOR✍

FRESH FISH

The quality of fish is largely determined by its freshness. Fresh fish should have the following characteristics:

1. Whole or dressed fish
   Skin should be shiny and bright, and scales should cling tightly.
   Gills should be a clear bright red, free from slime. In time the colour fades to a light pink, then grey and finally to brown or green.
   Eyes should be bright, clear and full. As fish loses its freshness, the eyes become faded and cloudy and tend to become sunken.
   Flesh should be firm and elastic to the touch and should not separate easily from the bone.
   Odour should be fresh and mild, not strong or fishy.
2. Fillets and steaks
   Flesh should be fresh cut in appearance and be the colour of freshly dressed fish. Texture should be firm. There should be no traces of browning about the edges or drying out of the flesh.
   Odour should be fresh and mild.
   Wrapped steaks and fillets should be packaged in moistureproof material, with little or no air space between the fish and the wrapping.

FRESH SHELLFISH

Shellfish deteriorate very rapidly, especially when shucked or removed from the shell. It is important that they be strictly fresh when purchased. If purchased in the shell, it is essential that they be alive or cooked.

Crab and lobster, when bought live, should show movement of the legs. When bought cooked, the shell should be a bright red and have a fresh, pleasant odour.

Shrimp and prawns should have a mild sea odour, and the meat should be firm in texture. The parchmentlike shell covering should fit tightly to the body; if the body has shrunk from the shell, the shrimp may not be fresh. The colour of the shell may vary from greyish-green to tan to light pink. If purchased cooked, the shell should be bright red. If buying shelled meat, it should be a distinctive pink, sometimes with red spots.

Live clams, oysters and mussels should have shells that are tightly closed or close on handling. A gaping shell indicates that it is dead and therefore not edible. Top quality oysters have hard, well-cupped shells.

Shucked oysters, clams and mussels should be plump and have a clear liquid. Note that mussel meat turns a bright orange when cooked.

Sea scallops should be creamy white, moist and have an agreeable odour. When halved, the fibres should be moist and full, not dried out.

Squid must have a fresh, moist appearance. Atlantic squid are white, Pacific squid are creamy white. There should be no strong odour.

COMMERCIALLY FROZEN FISH AND SHELLFISH

Commercially frozen fish and shellfish must be held constantly in the frozen state at –26°C (–15°F) or below. Changes in this storage temperature during transit or in retail storage cabinets will result in deterioration in quality. A check on the following points will ensure that fish has been properly handled.

Flesh should be solidly frozen and have a firm, glossy appearance, with no evidence of drying out such as white spots or papery corners and edges. There should be no dark spots, discolouration or fading of the flesh.

Frozen fillets, steaks and shellfish should be wrapped in moistureproof and vapourproof material. There should be little or no air space between the fish and the wrapping. A thick layer of frost on the inside of transparent wrappers is evidence of long storage or poor condition, or both. The majority of frozen fillets on the market are packaged in waxed cardboard boxes wrapped with waxed paper and are machine sealed. The consumer must rely on established brand names and the reputation of the retail outlet as assurances of quality.

Frozen whole or dressed fish are not usually wrapped. They should, however, be coated with a glaze of ice to prevent desiccation and discolouration.

PREPARATION
✿TECHNIQUES✿

These two drawings of whole flatfish and roundfish are for reference when preparing your catch or purchase.

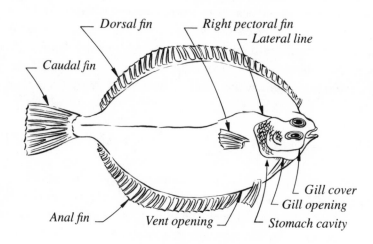

WHOLE FLATFISH

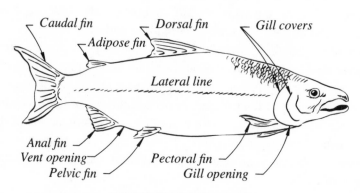

WHOLE ROUNDFISH

TO SCALE A FISH / TO CLEAN A WHOLE FISH

Grasp tail with one hand. Run knife's dull edge at 45° angle around fish.

Remove head by cutting around base of gills.

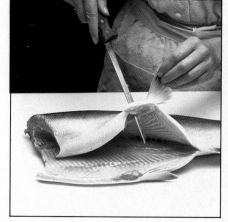

Remove pelvic fin by cutting around the attached muscle.

Remove dorsal fin by cutting against the direction in which it grows.

Remove remaining fins by cutting against the direction in which they grow.

To Bone a Fish For Stuffing

Cut through the ribs above the backbone, from head to tail.

Lay fish open and cut through ribs below the backbone, from head to tail.

Work entire backbone free and cut out, leaving back skin intact.

Remove belly bones on both sides.

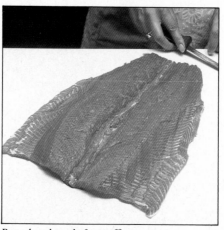

Boned and ready for stuffing.

To Fillet a Roundfish

Cut through the centre of the back down to backbone, from head to tail.

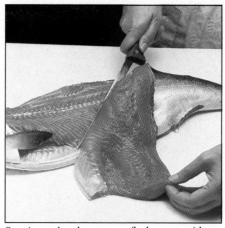

Starting at head, cut away flesh on one side of fish, from head to tail.

To Fillet a Flatfish / To Skin a Fillet

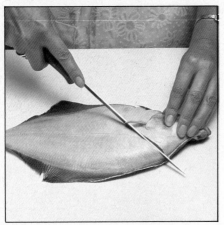

Make one side of deep V cut under head through to backbone, on one side of fish.

Use a gentle sawing motion to cut away flesh, from head to tail.

Turn fish over, make another V cut and remove the other fillet.

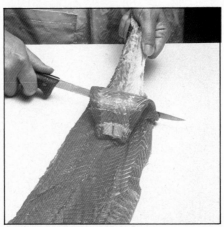

Cut skin away from flesh with knife at 45° angle towards the skin.

TO SHELL SHRIMP, PRAWNS / TO OPEN OYSTERS

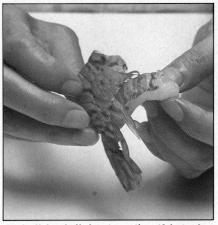

Use kitchen shears to cut through the soft undershell.

Peel off the shell, leaving tail on if desired.

Insert an oyster knife between the halves and use a twisting motion to pry apart.

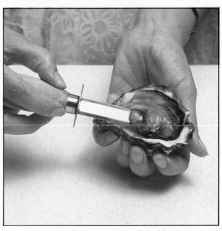

Sever the under muscle which holds the oyster to the shell.

TO CRACK LOBSTER

Use a heavy knife to break the body into parts, as shown.

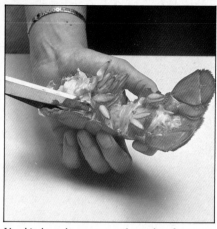

Use kitchen shears to cut through soft membrane on both sides under tail.

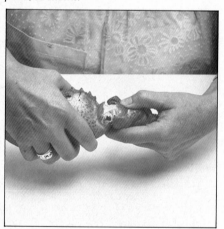

Use your hands to break apart each joint of the large claws.

Pull out the movable small pincer.

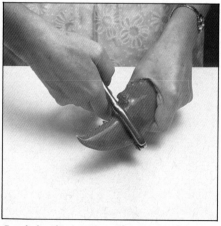

Crack the claws at the widest part, using a lobster cracker or nutcracker.

TO CRACK CRAB

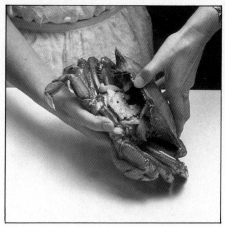

Pull off top shell.

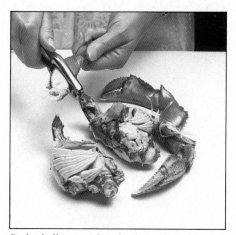

Body shell in two, legs broken off. Crack each section with a nutcracker.

TO PREPARE SQUID

Whole squid; finger pointing to end of the cellular backbone.

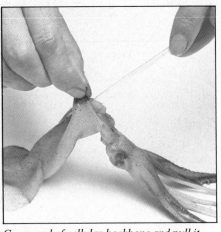

Grasp end of cellular backbone and pull it out.

Separate the body from the hood by gently pulling them apart.

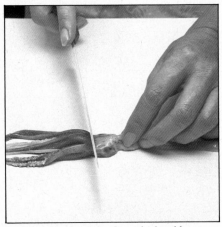

Separate the tentacles from the head by cutting apart just below the eyes.

Squeeze out and discard the hornlike beak from between the tentacles.

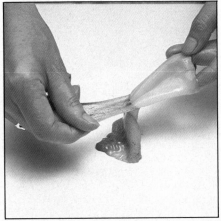

Pull off and discard the transparent, speckled membrane which covers the hood.

To Scale a Fish

Scaling may be done before or after dressing a fish. Use the dull edge of your knife or a fish scaler. Grasp the tail firmly with one hand and run the edge of the knife at a 45° angle from tail to head, all around the fish, until all scales are loosened. Do this under cold running water to prevent the scales from scattering about.

To Clean a Whole Fish

Cleaning consists of eviscerating or gutting the fish and washing it thoroughly. Use a thin, sharp knife (such as a filleting or boning knife) to slit the underbelly skin from vent to gills. Remove entrails. Wash fish in cold running water and use a soft brush to remove any remaining blood and viscera from the cavity. If blood is hard to remove, rub with table salt under cold running water.

To remove the head, cut around the base of the gills, keeping close to the hard collar bone. Make the same cut on both sides, then snap the backbone by bending it over the edge of the cutting board or table.

Remove pelvic fins by cutting around the attached muscle with a sharp knife. Remove dorsal fin by cutting against the direction in which it grows. Then remove the remaining fins in a similar manner.

Leave the tail on till the last, as it provides a convenient handle for scaling, filleting or skinning. To remove the tail, cut through the flesh and backbone just above the caudal fin.

To Bone a Fish For Stuffing

First, scale and clean the fish. Then continue the slit made from gills to vent to the tail. Grasp the fish firmly with one hand and hold the knife in your other hand. Insert the tip of a very sharp boning knife into the flesh above the backbone, cutting through the ribs down the length of the fish from head to tail. Keep close to the bones to avoid waste and take care to avoid cutting through the back skin.

Lay the fish open like a butterfly. This time, insert the knife below the backbone and cut through the ribs from head to tail, pressing up towards the bone to avoid waste.

Use the tip of the knife to work the entire backbone free and cut it out, leaving the back skin intact.

Remove the belly bones on both sides by inserting the knife under them, pressing up and easing them off the flesh with the blade while pulling the bones away with your other hand.

Now the fish is boned and ready for stuffing.

To Fillet a Roundfish

Before filleting, remove the scales unless the fish is going to be skinned. Use a very sharp filleting knife to pierce through the skin and flesh along the centre of the back to the backbone, cutting all the way from the tail to just below the head. With the knife held flat along the top of the backbone, start at the head and cut away the flesh on one side from head to tail, easing the knife over the rib bones. Remove the fillet. Turn the fish over and cut away the other fillet.

To Fillet a Flatfish

Use a sharp filleting knife to make one side of a deep V cut under the head and through to the backbone on one side of the flatfish. Make the cut for the other side of the V below the stomach cavity.

Hold the top edge of the fillet with one hand. With the other hand, press the knife flat against the rib bones and use a gentle sawing motion to remove the fillet, first off one side of the backbone, then the other. Turn the fish over, make another V cut and cut away the other fillet.

To Skin a Fillet

Place the fillet, skin side down, on the cutting board. Hold the tail firmly with one hand and cut the skin away from the flesh with quick, short strokes in a sawing motion. Slant the knife blade at a 45° angle towards the skin so that no flesh is wasted.

TO SHELL, DEVEIN AND COOK
SHRIMP AND PRAWNS

Shrimp and prawns may be cooked in the shell or after shelling and deveining. Be careful not to overcook, as the meat will become tough and dry.

To cook in the shell, bring water to the boil and add 25 mL (2 tbsp.) salt per litre (quart). Wash the shrimp and place in the boiling water. When water returns to the boil, reduce heat, cover and simmer. Small shrimp should be simmered 3 to 5 minutes, larger shrimp and prawns for 5 to 8 minutes. They are done when they curl up into a circle and turn bright red or pink. Drain and cool.

To shell and devein shrimp or prawns (cooked or raw), use a pair of kitchen shears to cut through the soft undershell of the shrimp and peel off the shell, leaving the tail on if desired. You may wish to loosen the sand vein (a dark thread) that runs down the centre of the back with the tip of a paring knife and rinse it off. The sand vein is not harmful and is often unnoticeable in small shrimp.

To cook without the shell, follow the directions given above to shell and devein the shrimp. Rinse under cold running water and cook as directed above or in a court bouillon (see index).

TO OPEN AND COOK OYSTERS

Before opening oysters, use a brush to scrub the shells clean under cold running water. Do not let the oysters stand in fresh water.

Hold the oyster with the deep half of the shell down in a folded cloth (or wear a heavy glove) in case the knife slips. Insert a strong, blunt oyster knife between the halves of the shell near the hinge, then use a twisting motion to pry the halves apart.

While opening the oyster, try to save as much of the delicious, natural liquid as possible. Once opened, slip the knife between the halves of the shell to sever the muscle that holds them together. Then sever the under muscle that holds the oyster to the shell. The oyster is now ready to be served.

If cooked oysters are required for use in a recipe, simmer in their own liquid until their edges begin to curl. This will take 2 to 4 minutes, depending on the size.

To Prepare, Cook and Crack Lobster

To cook lobster, bring to a boil in a large pan enough water to generously cover the lobster. Add 50 mL (¼ cup) salt to each 4.5 L (1 gal.) of water. Grasp the live lobster behind its head and plunge it head first into the boiling water. Cover the container and bring the water back to a boil. Reduce the heat and simmer. A 500 g (1 lb.) lobster will take 7 to 10 minutes; a 1 kg (2 lb.) lobster will take 10 to 15 minutes. Either serve at once or cool quickly under cold running water.

The meat may be removed most easily from the cooked lobster while it is still warm. Use a heavy knife to help break the body into parts as shown.

To remove the meat from the tail, cut through the soft membrane on both sides of the under shell with kitchen shears and lift out the meat in one piece. Snap off the flippers at the end of the tail, if desired, by bending them back.

Cut out and discard the dark intestinal vein that runs down the centre of the back. Remove the body shell by lifting it from the tail end. Discard the small, dark stomach sac or "lady" behind the head; either keep or discard the bright green "tomalley" (liver) and coral roe, if any. These may be used to make coral roe butter or tomalley spread (see index).

Use your hands to break apart each joint of the large claws and, with a toothpick or small fork, push out the meat in each section.

Pull out the small movable pincer, crack it and remove the meat.

To crack the claws, use a lobster cracker or nutcracker at the widest part. Apply enough force to break the shell but not enough to damage the meat, which may then be shaken from the shell.

Break off the small legs and extract the meat with a small fork or pick.

Serve the cracked lobster with melted butter and lemon wedges or use in any recipe calling for lobster meat.

To Prepare, Cook and Crack Crab

To cook crab, bring to a boil in a large pot enough water to cover the crab. Add 50 mL (¼ cup) salt for each 4.5 L (1 gal.) water. Plunge the live crab into the boiling water and cover. Return to the boil, then reduce heat and simmer for 10 to 20 minutes, depending on the size of the crab. One measuring 15 cm (6″) across the width of the shell should be ready in 10 minutes.

Remove crab and cool immediately under cold running water. Pull off top shell and either discard or scrub thoroughly for use as a serving container. Lift off gills on either side of the back and discard. Turn crab on its back and break off the mouth parts, tail or apron, and scrape out the entrails. Rinse thoroughly under cold running water.

Break the body shell in two and pick or shake out the body meat. Break off the legs. Pull out the movable small claws or pincer claws and the sharp cartilage. Break legs apart at joints, using a nutcracker gently to crack the hard shell of each section, and remove meat whole from each section.

Rinse the solid meat in salted water, drain and pat dry.

To serve the cracked crab, place the meat into the cleaned top shell and set on crushed ice. Arrange the cracked legs attractively around it. The meat may also be used in any recipe calling for crabmeat.

TO PREPARE AND COOK CLAMS OR MUSSELS

Scrub the shells with a brush under cold running water, then place in a steamer or sieve over rapidly boiling water. Cover tightly and steam until shells open. (Use a glass boiler—it is easier to check when the shells open.) Discard the shell and the "byssus" or black hair of mussels. Clams may be served on the half shell, if desired.

Serve with hot melted butter or use in any recipe calling for cooked clams or mussels.

TO PREPARE AND COOK SEA SCALLOPS

Fresh scallops may be cooked within a recipe such as Coquilles St. Jacques (see index). If the recipe calls for cooked scallops, wash fresh scallops under cold running water or partially thaw frozen scallops. If necessary, remove the tough, opaque bit of gristle sometimes present on the outer side of the scallop.

To cook, bring to a boil in a saucepan enough water to cover the scallops. Add 10 mL (2 tsp.) salt for each litre (quart) of water. Place scallops in the water and return to the boil. Cover and simmer for 3 to 4 minutes if fresh, 5 to 8 minutes if partially thawed.

TO PREPARE SQUID

Squid must be cleaned and prepared before cooking. Photo one shows the whole squid. A finger points to the end of the transparent cellular backbone. Grasp the end of the backbone and pull it out.

Separate the body from the hood by gently pulling them apart. Rinse the hood and keep it but discard the contents (body materials) of the hood, including the ink sac.

Separate the arms and tentacles from the head by cutting through them just below the eyes; discard the head. Squeeze out and discard the hornlike beak from between the tentacles.

Hold the hood under cold running water; pull off and discard the transparent speckled membrane which covers the hood.

Wash and dry the edible portions (hood and tentacles). Cut up or use whole as required in the recipe you are using.

TO SHUCK AND POUND ABALONE

To shuck and prepare live abalone, force a heavy wooden wedge between the meat and the shell. Move the wedge around until the meat falls from the shell. Cut off and discard the stomach sac on the side that was attached to the shell, being careful not to break the sac. Wash meat in cold running water. With a sharp knife, trim off dark portions around the edges of the meat. These may be used for chowder or fritters.

Hold the meat firmly on a board and use a thin, sharp knife, cutting across the grain (which runs lengthwise) to produce steaks about 1 cm (⅜″) thick. Pound each steak with a wooden mallet until limp and velvety. Use a light, rhythmical motion and pound evenly. If you prefer not to pound abalone, it may be put through a food chopper and minced. Generally, packaged frozen abalone steaks have been pounded sufficiently during processing and are ready for cooking after they have been thawed.

Storing Fish and Shellfish ✿In the Home✿

Refrigerator and Freezer Storage

Because fresh fish and shellfish spoil rapidly, care should be taken to serve them as soon as possible after purchase; the earlier they are served, the better the quality. The precautions outlined below will help to maintain quality when holding them in the refrigerator for even short periods.

Fresh fish should be unwrapped and wiped with a clean damp cloth as soon as you get it home. If the fish is whole, eviscerate it immediately. Wrap in waxed paper, place in a tightly covered container to prevent transfer of odours and store in the refrigerator. Keep no longer than two days.

Fresh shellfish should be used as quickly as possible. Crab, lobster, oysters, clams or mussels purchased live may be kept alive covered with a damp cloth or layer of seaweed in the refrigerator or other cool place for up to 12 hours. Do not store live lobster or crab on ice or in fresh water. Cooked or fresh shellfish and shucked oysters, clams or mussels may be kept no longer than 1 to 2 days in the refrigerator at 5°C (40°F) unless otherwise stated. Cartons containing fresh molluscs should be refrigerated or surrounded by ice until used. Oysters, if kept at temperatures above freezing and below 4° C (40° F), will remain alive for up to 10 days. Clams and mussels will keep for 3 to 4 days at these temperatures.

Commercially frozen fish and shellfish should be kept solidly frozen in the unopened package. A constant temperature of –23°C (–15°F) is required to maintain quality but this is hard to do in home freezer units, so it is advisable to keep such products for relatively short periods. The general guidelines in the freezer storage timetable refer to products frozen commercially or under ideal conditions with subsequent constant low-temperature storage in a home freezer (not a top-of-refrigerator freezer). The timetable does not take into account the variables attributable to the freshness of products when purchased.

Commercially smoked fish (fresh or frozen) should be handled and stored in the same way as fresh or frozen fish.

Once fish or shellfish has been thawed, it must be used quickly, since it will spoil as readily as the fresh product. It is recommended not to refreeze raw fish which has been thawed. However, thawed fish may be cooked and frozen for a short period.

No home freezing of fish can equal the speed and low temperature of commercial feezing. Therefore, home-frozen fish and shellfish should not be stored for as long as the times given in the timetable. (See section on home freezing.)

FREEZER STORAGE TIMETABLE

PRODUCT	COMMENTS	MAXIMUM STORAGE TIME
Whole fish	Frozen in an ice block or commercially ice glazed	6 months
Whole fish	Wrapped in freezer paper	3 to 4 months
Fish fillets	Commercially frozen	2 to 3 months
Fish steaks	Commercially frozen	2 to 3 months
Oysters Mussels Clams Scallops	Commercially frozen (shucked)	3 to 4 months
Crab Lobster Shrimp Squid	Commercially frozen	1 to 2 months

HOME FREEZING

1. Fish

   Freshly caught fish may be frozen and stored in the home freezer. It should be eviscerated and washed soon after it is caught. If there is to be any delay before freezing, pack it in ice or store in the refrigerator for no longer than 8 hours to ensure maximum quality. Do not home freeze store-bought fresh fish.

   Fish may be packed dressed, filleted or cut into steaks. Before packing, rinse the fish in a cold brine solution of 250 mL (1 cup) pickling salt to 4.5 L (1 gal.) water—or a 2 per cent ascorbic acid solution of 10 mL (2 tsp.) to 1 L (1 qt.) cold water. Either may be used to delay rancidity in fatty fish. To prevent deterioration as a result of drying or oxidation, wrap in moistureproof and vapourproof material, packing tightly to exclude air. Heavy aluminum foil, vapourproof cellophane, pliofilm, polyethylene or laminated freezer paper all make satisfactory packaging materials. Label with the date.

   Freeze quickly at low temperature to maintain quality, then store at a constant temperature of at least –18°C (0°F), lower if possible. Lean fish will keep well for 2 to 3 months. Fatty fish should not be kept for more than 1 to 2 months. Frozen home-smoked fish will keep for 3 to 4 weeks. Frozen fish stored for longer will still be safe to eat but will begin to lose its freshness, may develop rancidity and will slowly deteriorate.

2. Shellfish

   All shellfish, like fish, should be frozen quickly at as low a temperature as possible, then stored at a constant temperature of at least –18°C (0°F), lower if possible. Remember to label with the date.

   Oysters, clams and mussels should not be frozen in the shell. They should be shucked and packed in their liquid in containers. Cover completely to prevent darkening; crushed cellophane or foil in the top of the container will help to keep them covered with liquid.

   Squid and scallops should be washed in brine (using same formula as for fish), drained, then packed in freezer bags. Exclude as much air as possible and seal tightly.

   Lobster, crab, shrimp and squid may be frozen but tend to toughen in storage and should not be kept for longer than one month. Pack the cold cooked meat in freezer containers in small amounts (enough to be used at one time). Pour in enough cold brine to cover. To make brine, use 10 mL (2 tsp.) pickling salt for each 250 mL (1 cup) water. Allow 1.25 cm (½″) headspace and fasten lids securely.

HOME CANNING

GENERAL RULES

WARNING: INFORMATION GIVEN HERE MUST BE STRICTLY ADHERED TO IN ORDER TO PROVIDE A SAFE PRODUCT.

Since the author and publisher have no control over the many variables that may be present, such as freshness of fish or individual standards of hygiene, we disclaim any responsibility for damage or illness resulting from any person's interpretation of these rules.

Canning is a popular method employed by many homemakers to preserve surplus fish. The result can be delicious, but, as anyone familiar with canning knows, it can also be dangerous, even deadly, if proper procedures are not followed. The reason for concern is that several deaths occur each year from botulism contracted through consumption of improperly home-canned fish or other food.

Botulism food poisoning, which is often fatal, is a result of consuming food containing the toxin produced by the micro-organism *Clostridium botulinum*. This is the most potentially dangerous of all food spoilage organisms and also one of the most difficult to destroy. It thrives at room temperature, in the absence of air and in a moist environment, conditions that exist in combination in a container of canned fish. Although the toxin produced by the organism can be destroyed by subjecting it to a temperature of 100°C (212°F) for a relatively short period of time, the spore itself is much more heat resistant, requiring exposure to a temperature of 116°C (240°F) or higher for a sustained period of time to ensure complete destruction. This can be achieved only through canning under pressure for the required time.

Since the toxin can cause death and is destroyed readily by heating at 100°C (212°F), it is recommended home-canned fish should be heated in an open saucepan to boiling and boiled for 20 minutes, before tasting it. If there is any evidence of bad odours or foaming, it should be destroyed so that it cannot be consumed by people or animals.

Canning fish relies on two fundamental procedures:

1. the exclusion of air, thus creating a vacuum and sealing the food in the container away from outside contamination during storage; and
2. heat sterilization to destroy spoilage organisms, thus ensuring the food safety of the canned fish. This can only be accomplished by heating the exhausted, sealed container in a pressure canner for a specified time at a specified pressure.

Using any other method to can fish, including open kettle canning, water bath canning and oven canning, is unsafe and can result in serious or even fatal food poisoning.

Shellfish should not be canned as it is more perishable than fish; also, it is impossible to duplicate the controlled conditions necessary for commercial canning.

Normally, salmon, trout and tuna are the only fish that should be canned in the home.

Because of the potential for food poisoning with home canning, special care must be taken to follow closely the general procedures set out in this section. The specific procedures for salmon and trout vary from those for tuna, as tuna must be cooked before canning.

To home can fish safely, the special items noted below will be required:

1. Steam pressure canner

    DO NOT USE SMALL PRESSURE COOKERS as these are intended only for cooking loose food, not canning.

    Steam pressure canners are obtainable in several sizes and are generally made of cast aluminum. The body of the canner is fitted with a cover which is designed to clamp on in a locking position for steam pressure processing. The cover is equipped with a dial-type pressure gauge or rocker gauge, which indicates pressure in pounds per square inch (kilopascals) and sometimes the corresponding temperature equivalents. Also, the cover has a vent opening, with a removable pressure control weighted cap, to vent air and steam. Before commencing pressure processing, the cap is not in place; when beginning pressure processing, the cap is put in place. In the event that the pressure gets too high for safety, the cover has an automatic air vent or safety valve to release excess steam.

    It is recommended that a canner with a capacity of at least 15 L (13.3 imp. qt. or 16 U.S. qt.) be used. This size will accommodate nine 455 mL (1 pt./16 oz.) glass jars. If a substantial amount of fish is to be canned, a larger size of canner may be preferable in order to minimize the labour and cost.

    Read your pressure canner instruction manual with care to fully understand its operation and other imperatives, such as its cleaning and care, as well as the pressure or rocker gauge allowance that must be made for processing at different altitudes. For example, 8 oz. (3.5 kPa) should be added to the pressure gauge for every 310 m (1000′) of your location above sea level. Remember to have the pressure gauge tested for accuracy at least once a year.

2. Glass jars

Only jars of 228 or 455 mL (½ or 1 pt./8 or 16 oz.) size, specially made for home pressure canning, should be used. These should be of the "mason" type, with a screw band and metal lid, preferably with straight sides and a wide mouth opening. (Glass lids are not recommended.) Before use, jars and lids should be inspected for defects, particularly around the rims. If any nicks or chips are evident, however small, the container should be discarded.

Metal cans are not recommended for home canning for a number of reasons. They must be specially ordered from a can manufacturer, whereas glass jars are readily available from supermarkets and hardware stores. Moreover, glass jars (unlike metal cans) are reusable. To seal the can lid, a special—and costly—seaming machine is needed. Also, knowledge and training are necessary to enable an operator to evaluate the safety of a can seam and to make any necessary adjustments to the machine.

3. Timer

An accurate alarm clock or oven timer is required to time the heat processing.

4. Thermometer

An accurate thermometer is required to check the temperature of the packed fish during precooking or "exhausting."

PROCESSING SALMON AND TROUT

Before proceeding, please read the general rules on home canning.

1. Sterilize the jars. Wash jars, screw bands and lids thoroughly in hot soapy water and rinse well with scalding water. Place all pieces in a container and keep covered with scalding water until required.

2. Prepare the fish. Use only absolutely fresh fish of good quality. If the fish must be kept for more than three hours after it is caught, clean and gut it, then pack in ice or refrigerate. Smoked fish must be canned as soon as it has cooled after the smoking process, following the same procedure as for fresh fish; add 15 minutes to the processing time.

Scrub fish with coarse salt and a cloth to remove any film and loose scales. Remove scales, fins, head and tail, then gut thoroughly. The backbone need not be removed. (It softens during processing, becoming quite edible, and contains valuable calcium and other nutrients which would otherwise be lost.) Rinse the fish well, inside and out, with cold running water.

3. Pack the jars. Do not mix sizes of jars in a batch and do not pack more jars than can be processed at one time. Cut the fish into pieces suitable for the size of jars you are using. For large fish, fillet pieces are easier to pack than steaks. Pack the pieces solidly in the jars, with the skin side next to the glass. Carefully fill any voids with trimmed pieces. Leave 1.5 mm (⅟₁₆″) headspace below the top of the rim.

4. Salting. Add 2.5 mL (½ tsp.) of pickling salt to each packed 228 mL (½ pt./8 oz.) jar, 5 mL (1 tsp.) to each 455 mL (1 pt./16 oz.) jar.

5. Exhausting. Place metal lids on packed jars and twist down the screw bands part way, just enough so that they cannot be pulled off. This half-closing procedure is necessary to allow air to escape from the container during exhausting. Place jars on a wire rack in the bottom of the canner and pour hot water around them to a level halfway up the sides of the jars. Put the cover on the pressure canner but do not place the cap over the vent.

    Turn the heat on high under the pressure canner until the water is boiling, as evidenced by a strong continuous flow of steam coming from the vent. Reduce the heat slightly but maintain boiling for 10 to 20 minutes until a minimum temperature of 77°C (170°F) is reached in the packed fish pieces closest to the centre of the jars. To check the temperature, remove the cover from the pressure canner, open a test jar and insert the bulb of a sterilized thermometer into the centre of the packed fish.

6. Pressure processing. When exhausting is complete, remove canner from heat. Remove jars singly and twist down screw bands until firmly tight, then replace in canner. The hot water remaining in the canner following exhausting should be adequate for pressure canning. If necessary, add boiling water to bring the level to one-third the height of the jars. Replace cover of canner, making sure it is turned completely into the locking position. Do not place cap over vent.

    Turn heat on high under canner until a strong steady flow of steam comes from the vent and allow this to continue for 10 minutes. Close the vent by placing the cap over it, thus increasing pressure inside the canner. When the pressure or rocker gauge indicates 10 lbs. (70 kPa), commence timing. This pressure must be maintained constantly for 110 minutes.

    If the pressure drops during this period, it must be brought back up to 10 lbs. (70 kPa), and the timing restarted. Obviously, this will result in the fish being overcooked, so it is important to monitor the pressure carefully throughout the pressure processing.

7. Cooling. At the conclusion of the timing period, turn off the heat. Do not attempt to remove the pressure canner cover until the pressure gauge has returned to zero. Remove processed jars carefully and allow them to air cool at room temperature.

8. Check closure seals. When the jars cool, the metal lids will snap down and become concave, indicating a vacuum and a good seal. If any lid is not concave, press down its centre with your thumb. If the lid springs back up, the seal has been broken and the container must not be stored. The fish in the jar may be refrigerated and treated as any other cooked fish; remember to use within one to two days.

   If the lid remains concave, the seal is probably intact but should be tested. Remove the screw band, grasp the lid by its edges and lift up the jar a few inches. If the seal is weak, the lid will come off the jar. Should this happen, refrigerate the contents of the jar (as above). If the seal holds tight, replace the screw band and store the canned fish for future use.

9. Storing. Processed jars of fish should be stored in a cool 0° to 10°C (32° to 50°F) dark storage area until required. Storage life is up to one year.

PROCESSING TUNA

Before proceeding, please read the general rules on home canning for general directions. Tuna, like salmon and trout, must be canned under pressure to destroy spoilage organisms and ensure its safety.

   Canning tuna is time consuming and requires more effort than salmon or trout, since it must be cooked before canning. Either fresh or frozen tuna may be canned. Frozen tuna must be completely thawed in the refrigerator prior to processing; otherwise, its temperature may be too low for safety.

1. Prepare the tuna. Clean the fish thoroughly and remove its entrails. If large, remove the head and tail. Rinse the stomach cavity with cold running water and allow to drain.

   Place fish, gut cavity down, on a metal tray or perforated pan with legs. If necessary, cut the fish into pieces across the round. Lower into the pressure canner, making sure that fish is raised above the water level.

   Cook at 100° to 102°C (212° to 216°F) for 2 to 3½ hours, depending on the weight of the tuna; a 5 kg (11 lb.) fish will take about two hours.

This precooking must be done to remove the bitter oils present in the tuna's flesh. Allow fish to cool for two hours at room temperature, then refrigerate below 0°C (32°F) for 12 to 24 hours.

2. Sterilize the jars. Follow the instructions given in step 1 under processing salmon and trout.
3. Pack the jars. Peel off the skin with a knife, lightly scraping the surface to remove any blood vessels. Break fish apart into two halves, from back to belly. Remove backbone. Cut halves in two. Pull off and cut out all bones and fin bases. Scrape and cut off dark flesh, leaving four clean all-white meat sections.

   Cut sections crosswise into lengths to fit 228 mL (½ pt./8 oz.) jars; anything larger is not recommended. Leave 2.5 cm (1″) headspace and gently press down meat make a solid pack.

   To each jar, add 2 mL (½ tsp.) pickling salt and 50 mL (4 tbsp.) vegetable oil.
4. Exhausting. Follow the instructions given in step 5 under processing salmon and trout. Then wipe off any fat from the jars and lids.
5. Pressure processing. Follow the instructions given in step 6 under processing salmon and trout. Start timing when the pressure or rocker gauge indicates 10 lbs. (70 kPa), 116°C (240°F) and maintain for 110 minutes.
6. Cooling. Follow the instructions given in step 7 under processing salmon and trout.
7. Check closure seals. Follow the instructions given in step 8 under processing salmon and trout.
8. Storing. Wrap jars in brown paper or store in cartons to exclude as much light as possible, since exposure to light can cause rancidity.

HOME SMOKING

The Indians have used this method of preserving fish for hundreds of years and still use many of the same techniques handed down through the generations. Because it results in an unusual, mouth-watering taste, the smoking of fish is becoming a very popular method of preservation. Although preservation by smoking usually lasts for a shorter time than by salting, the product is more appetizing. When the curing is properly done, the product is of high quality and attractive in both appearance and taste. The efficiency of smoking depends on the drying action of a smouldering fire. Wood smoke has little if any preservative action; it is only a flavouring and colouring agent.

Here again, the potential danger of botulism food poisoning must be recognized. The organism *Clostridium botulinum* is able to survive and grow at temperatures higher than 3°C (37.5°F) in the absence of air. Therefore, always avoid these conditions by storing smoked fish at 3°C (37.5°F) or lower and never package so as to exclude air (do not use vacuum packaging). Finally, never omit the salting step in the process, as salt inhibits the growth of this dangerous organism.

Depending on the species, fish may be smoked in the round (gutted), split and beheaded, or in pieces (with or without the skin).

There are two basic methods of smoking: hot and cold. In a hot smoking or smoke cooking process, the fish is dried for a short period, then exposed to a relatively low-temperature smoke to develop a good flavour; the temperature is increased towards the latter part of the process to cook the fish, yielding a cooked or semicooked product, depending on the length of the process. Fish smoked this way is ready to eat and makes delicious eating hot or cold; it is virtually a smoked, barbecued product.

With cold smoking, the fish is smoked at low temperature for a relatively long period of time, yielding an uncooked product. This method takes longer than hot smoking but the fish keeps longer. Depending on the type of product, cold-smoked fish may be eaten uncooked or may require cooking before serving.

One type of long, low-temperature smoking given to sides of salmon results in the world-renowned delicacy called lox, which is served without cooking. On the other hand, kippers or smoked herring are produced by a low-temperature smoking process but require cooking before eating.

Some of the factors that will influence the choice between hot and cold smoking are the type of product desired, the fish species, the form in which the fish was initially processed, and the type of smoking equipment available.

HOT SMOKING OR SMOKE COOKING

The two methods of hot smoking described below are designed for use with the portable hot-smoke cooker illustrated here. Other types of hot-smoking kilns may be used but they would, of course, require different methods of adjustment to control temperature and would probably require some adjustment in the smoking times to obtain a similar finished product. These methods may be used with almost any species, including salmon, trout, shad, mackerel, herring, lake whitefish, tullibee and sablefish (Alaska black cod).

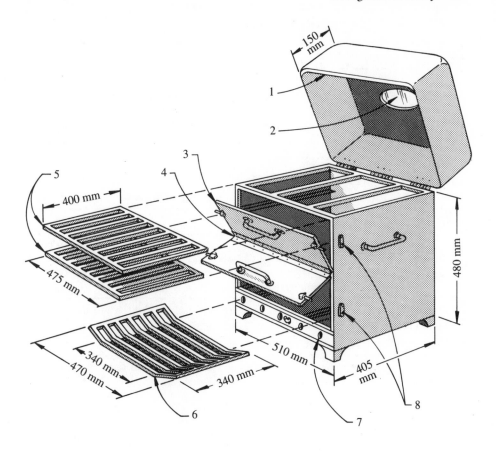

PORTABLE HOT-SMOKE COOKER

The cooker sections are constructed of 16-gauge aluminum sheet metal, attached to an inner frame of angle iron, 12 mm × 12 mm × 3 mm (½″ × ½″ × ⅛″)

1. *Lip* (for lifting lid): 25 mm (1″)
2. *Vent* (slides open): to control smoke density and temperature, 100 mm (4″) in diameter
3. *Door* opens down to horizontal position to enable cooker to be used as a conventional barbecue by placing a grill on one of the lower grill supports
4. *Hinge*
5. *Cooking grills:* 475 mm × 400 mm (18¾″ × 15¾″)
6. *Fire support:* 470 mm × 340 mm (18½″ × 13½″)
7. *Vent slide* (adjustable) to control fire-burning rate
8. *Catches* to secure doors

HOT SMOKING TIMETABLE

METHOD 1 (dressed fish)

WEIGHT RANGE grams (pounds)	BRINING TIME* (minutes)	DRYING TIME (minutes)	SMOKE COOKING TIME* (hours)
112 to 340 (¼ to ¾)	15 to 20	60 to 90	1 to 1½
340 to 562 (¾ to 1¼)	25 to 40	60 to 90	1½ to 2
562 to 900 (1¼ to 2)	40 to 60	60 to 90	2 to 2⅔
900 to 1575 (2 to 3½)	60 to 90	60 to 90	2¾ to 4

METHOD 2 (fillets)

WEIGHT RANGE grams (pounds)	DRY SALTING TIME* (minutes)	MARINATING TIME (minutes)	DRYING TIME (minutes)	SMOKE COOKING TIME* (hours)
112 to 225 (¼ to ½)	20	30	30 to 60	1 to 1½
225 to 340 (½ to ¾)	30	30	30 to 60	1½
340 to 450 (¾ to 1)	40	30	30 to 60	1½ to 2

* These times are suggested as a guide only and can be adjusted to suit individual taste preferences.

METHOD ONE (DRESSED FISH)

1. Prepare the fish. Clean, dress and scale fish. Remove the head, tail and all fins. To facilitate salt and smoke flavour penetration, particularly with larger fish, make shallow surface incisions 3 to 5 mm (⅛ to ¼″) deep on both sides of the fish, and one incision of a similar depth down the centre of the back.
2. Brining. Prepare a brine solution by adding 1 kg (4 cups) of pickling salt—do not use iodized table salt—to 4.5 L (1 gal.) of water, stirring until completely dissolved. This amount of brine will be sufficient for about 4.5 kg (10 lbs.) of fish.

   Immerse the fish in the brine for the length of time specified in the hot-smoking timetable. Remove the fish and rinse briefly with a light spray of fresh water to remove surface salt.
3. Drying. Place fish on a wire rack in a cool, shaded, screened area, preferably in a light breeze, for 60 to 90 minutes to allow surface drying to take place. During the brining, salt was absorbed into the flesh; besides imparting flavour, it also swelled the protein and caused some to be dissolved into the brine, leaving a slightly sticky coating on the fish, particularly on the cut flesh surfaces. On drying, this sticky coating of protein forms a "pellicle" or gloss which takes on an attractive colouration when the fish is smoked.
4. Hot smoking. While the fish are drying, remove the grills from the smoke cooker and prepare a fire in its base on the fire support. Lay a small heap of charcoal briquets, saturate with starter fluid and light. When the charcoal is burning well and is covered with a grey ash, cover it with a layer of dampened wood chips, sawdust, small broken twigs or bark to develop a dense smoke. Smoke density and/or flaming can be controlled by using a water-filled mist-spraying bottle. The fuel-burning rate and the temperature can be regulated by adjusting the front base slide vent and the lid vent.

   After the drying period, lay the fish on cold clean grills previously treated with a spray-on nonstick vegetable oil coating. Place the grills on the surface position of the cooker and the highest lower grill support and close the lid. See the timetable; times given may vary, depending on how carefully the fuel-burning rate is regulated. During the initial period of smoke cooking, high smoke density should be maintained, along with a relatively low temperature. This can be accomplished by adjusting the base slide vent to a nearly closed position and the lid vent to an open position. During the latter period of smoke cooking, the surface temperature should be increased by opening the base slide vent more and nearly closing the lid vent to allow the fish to cook. Also during the latter period the fish should be turned over on the grills, and the positions of the grills exchanged.

5. Storing. May be stored in the refrigerator for 2 to 3 days. If longer storage is required, wrap the individual fish tightly in freezer paper and freeze; keeps 3 to 4 weeks.

6. Serving. Fish prepared this way is delicious eaten immediately after smoking, or serve chilled with a salad.

METHOD TWO (FILLETS)

This method uses a dry salting procedure instead of a brine treatment, followed by marinating before drying and hot smoking. Use fillets that have had the scales removed but not the skin.

1. Salting. Use 135 g (½ cup) of fine, high-grade pickling salt—do not use iodized table salt—to 2.25 kg (5 lbs.) of fillets. Lay the fillets skin side down on a clean dry surface previously sprinkled with about one-quarter of the salt. Evenly apply the remainder of the salt to the flesh surface. Allow the fillets to absorb the salt for the time specified in the hot-smoking timetable. Rinse both sides of the fillets with a gentle spray of fresh water to remove surface salt.

2. Marinating. Measure the following ingredients into a 500 mL (1 pt./16 oz.) screw-top jar:

375 mL	soy sauce	1½ cups
75 mL	dry sherry	6 Tbsp.
25 mL	sesame oil	2 Tbsp.
10 mL	sugar	2 tsp.
5 mL	ginger powder	1 tsp.

Close jar securely and shake well until thoroughly mixed.

Place the rinsed, salted fillets in a container just large enough to hold them but with enough remaining space to allow the fillets to be surrounded by the marinade. (A plastic bag is excellent for this purpose, because air and insects—if the fish is being prepared outdoors—can readily be excluded by closing the bag with a twist-tie. Also, the fillets will be well immersed in the marinade at all times.) Pour the marinade over the fillets, cover and refrigerate or place in a cool, shaded area. Leave for the time specified in the timetable.

3. Drying. Remove the fillets from marinade and drain briefly to remove

excess liquid. Place on a wire rack in a cool, shaded, screened area to dry as in method one.

4. Hot smoking. After drying, lay the fillets skin side down on cold, clean grills previously treated with a spray-on nonstick vegetable oil coating. Smoke cook as in method one but do not turn fillets over. For smoking times, see timetable.

5. Storing. Smoked fillets may be stored in the refrigerator for 2 or 3 days. If longer storage is required, wrap individual fillets tightly in freezer paper; keeps for 3 to 4 weeks.

6. Serving. May be served immediately after smoking or chilled with a salad.

COLD SMOKING

There are two basic methods of cold smoking. One yields a product that will require cooking before eating; the other, lengthier procedure yields a product that is saltier, drier and eaten uncooked.

The kiln used for cold smoking is designed so that the smoke producer is remote from the cabinet that holds the fish. This allows the smoke to cool before entering the cabinet. Relative humidity, an important factor in the control of moisture content in the fish, can be regulated by adjusting the amount of air entering the transitory duct. Ideally, a relative humidity of 60 to 70 per cent should be maintained. However, without instruments to measure humidity, experience and familiarity with the particular kiln being used and the quality of the final product will key the operator in selecting the settings to control air entry. It should be noted that the total fish load smoked in any kiln represents a large amount of water, since most fish contains about 80 per cent moisture.

In the early stages of smoking, the air entry shutter should be fully open to effect drying and consequent moisture reduction. Later in the smoking process, the air entry shutter can be partially closed to maintain the surface pellicle without excessive drying and also to facilitate smoke flavour absorption. If it is necessary to increase the velocity of the air to effect drying and moisture reduction in the initial stages (weather at time of smoking will be the principal factor), an exhaust fan can be installed at point B as shown in the drawing of a cold-smoking kiln.

If you are constructing a cold-smoking kiln from material such as an old refrigerator or a wooden or metal barrel, make sure that the smoke source is remote from the smoking cabinet to maintain the low temperature necessary for cold smoking. This temperature should be about 30°C (85°F) and should not exceed 32°C (90°F).

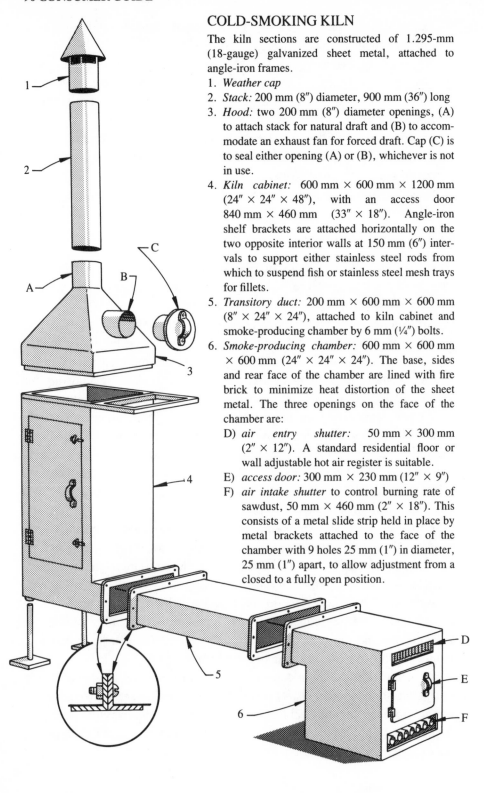

COLD-SMOKING KILN

The kiln sections are constructed of 1.295-mm (18-gauge) galvanized sheet metal, attached to angle-iron frames.

1. *Weather cap*
2. *Stack:* 200 mm (8″) diameter, 900 mm (36″) long
3. *Hood:* two 200 mm (8″) diameter openings, (A) to attach stack for natural draft and (B) to accommodate an exhaust fan for forced draft. Cap (C) is to seal either opening (A) or (B), whichever is not in use.
4. *Kiln cabinet:* 600 mm × 600 mm × 1200 mm (24″ × 24″ × 48″), with an access door 840 mm × 460 mm (33″ × 18″). Angle-iron shelf brackets are attached horizontally on the two opposite interior walls at 150 mm (6″) intervals to support either stainless steel rods from which to suspend fish or stainless steel mesh trays for fillets.
5. *Transitory duct:* 200 mm × 600 mm × 600 mm (8″ × 24″ × 24″), attached to kiln cabinet and smoke-producing chamber by 6 mm (¼″) bolts.
6. *Smoke-producing chamber:* 600 mm × 600 mm × 600 mm (24″ × 24″ × 24″). The base, sides and rear face of the chamber are lined with fire brick to minimize heat distortion of the sheet metal. The three openings on the face of the chamber are:
   D) *air entry shutter:* 50 mm × 300 mm (2″ × 12″). A standard residential floor or wall adjustable hot air register is suitable.
   E) *access door:* 300 mm × 230 mm (12″ × 9″)
   F) *air intake shutter* to control burning rate of sawdust, 50 mm × 460 mm (2″ × 18″). This consists of a metal slide strip held in place by metal brackets attached to the face of the chamber with 9 holes 25 mm (1″) in diameter, 25 mm (1″) apart, to allow adjustment from a closed to a fully open position.

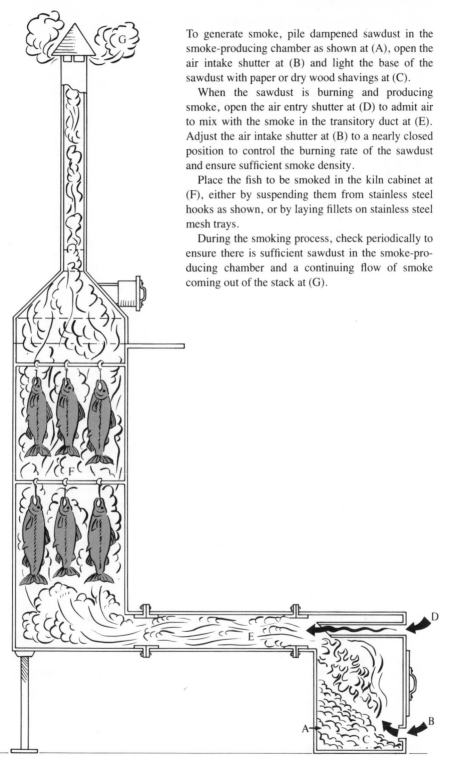

To generate smoke, pile dampened sawdust in the smoke-producing chamber as shown at (A), open the air intake shutter at (B) and light the base of the sawdust with paper or dry wood shavings at (C).

When the sawdust is burning and producing smoke, open the air entry shutter at (D) to admit air to mix with the smoke in the transitory duct at (E). Adjust the air intake shutter at (B) to a nearly closed position to control the burning rate of the sawdust and ensure sufficient smoke density.

Place the fish to be smoked in the kiln cabinet at (F), either by suspending them from stainless steel hooks as shown, or by laying fillets on stainless steel mesh trays.

During the smoking process, check periodically to ensure there is sufficient sawdust in the smoke-producing chamber and a continuing flow of smoke coming out of the stack at (G).

COLD SMOKING TIMETABLE

METHOD 1 (dressed fish)				
WEIGHT RANGE grams (pounds)	BRINING TIME* (minutes)	DRYING TIME (minutes)	SMOKING TIME* (hours)	SMOKING TEMPERATURES Celsius (Fahrenheit)
112 to 340 (¼ to ¾)	20 to 40	60 to 90	4½ to 5½	30° to 32° (85° to 90°)
340 to 562 (¾ to 1¼)	40 to 60	60 to 90	5½ to 6	30° to 32° (85° to 90°)
562 to 900 (1¼ to 2)	60 to 90	60 to 90	6	30° to 32° (85° to 90°)
METHOD 2 (fillets)				
WEIGHT RANGE grams (pounds)	SALTING TIME* (hours)	DRYING TIME (hours)	SMOKING TIME* (hours)	SMOKE TEMPERATURES Celsius (Fahrenheit)
675 to 900 (1½ to 2)	4 to 5	6 to 8	6 to 8	26.5° to 29.5° (80° to 85°)
900 to 1350 (2 to 3)	5 to 7	8 to 12	8	26.5° to 29.5° (80° to 85°)
1350 to 2250 (3 to 5)	7 to 9	8 to 12	8	26.5° to 29.5° (80° to 85°)

* These times are suggested as a guide only and can be adjusted to suit individual taste preferences.

METHOD ONE (DRESSED FISH)

This method of cold smoking yields a product that requires cooking before eating. Appropriate species include salmon, shad, herring, mackerel, lake whitefish, goldeye, tullibee, lake trout, rainbow trout and northern pike.

1. Prepare the fish. Clean, dress and scale the fish. Leave on the head and tail; with some species, these are the strongest points from which to suspend the fish during smoking.
2. Brining. Prepare a brine solution by adding 1 kg (4 cups) of pickling salt—do not use iodized table salt—to 4.5 L (1 gal.) water and stir until completely dissolved. Use 4.5 L (1 gal.) of brine to 4.5 kg (10 lbs.) of fish.

    Immerse the fish in the brine for the time specified in the cold-smoking timetable. Remove the fish and rinse briefly with a light spray of fresh water to remove surface salt.
3. Drying. Place fish on a wire rack in a cool, shaded, screened area, preferably in a light breeze, for about 60 to 90 minutes to allow surface drying to take place. Alternatively, if the smoking kiln is fitted with an exhaust fan, the fish can be hung in the cabinet, and surface drying can be effected with the fan in operation and the air entry shutter open.

4. Cold smoking. Insert S-shaped, stainless steel hooks in the tail or head section of the fish and suspend in the cabinet as shown in the drawing of the cold-smoking kiln. Prepare a fire in the smoke producer section of the kiln. For smoking times refer to timetable.
5. Storing. If the fish are to be cooked within 2 to 3 days after smoke processing, store in the refrigerator. If longer storage is required, wrap each piece individually in freezer paper and freeze for later use. Frozen smoked fish may be stored 3 to 4 weeks.
6. Serving. Thaw frozen smoked fish overnight at refrigerator temperature. Make an incision down the centre of the back of the fish, 5 mm (¼") deep, with the tip of a sharp knife. Wrap fish individually in aluminum foil and bake 20 to 35 minutes in an oven preheated to 204°C (400°F).

METHOD TWO (FILLETS)

This cold-smoking procedure yields a product that does not have to be cooked before eating. It is generally applied to fillets of salmon, but good results can also be obtained with lake trout, arctic charr and inconnu, which are fairly fatty species. The fillets should be generally 675 g (1.5 lbs.) or larger.

If you plan to suspend the fish in the kiln cabinet, carefully remove the head so as to leave the collarbone intact. The fillet can then be suspended from the collarbone by inserting three to four hooks below the bone.

Alternatively, the fillets can be laid skin side down on stainless steel mesh trays previously treated with a spray-on nonstick vegetable oil coating. Since the fillets will be cold smoked, the problem of fish cooking onto the trays (experienced with hot smoking) should not occur. If this alternative method is used, the collarbone can be cut away from the fillet.

The ribcage bones can be left in place during the initial fillet preparation if desired. They are sometimes left in place commercially to minimize "gaping" in the cut flesh surface, a condition in which the connected muscle segments separate, detracting from the final appearance. However, gaping should not occur in fish of high quality. Finally, the skin should be scored lightly with the tip of a sharp knife at the thickest part of the fillet to allow more even salt penetration.

1. Salting. Use about 350 g (1⅓ cups) of pickling salt to every 4.5 kg (10 lbs.) of fillets. Slightly more or less salt can be used, depending on individual tastes. The salt can also be supplemented with brown or white sugar, white pepper and/or ground cloves, which should be blended well with the salt before use.

Lay the fillets skin side down on a clean, dry surface previously sprinkled evenly with about one-third of the salt or salt-and-seasoning mixture. Apply the remainder evenly to the flesh surface. Allow the fillets to salt cure for the time specified in the cold-smoking timetable. Rinse with a light spray of fresh water to remove surface salt.

2. Drying. This method requires a considerably longer drying period than the previously described ones. Since the final product is eaten uncooked, it is necessary to reduce the moisture content sufficiently to yield a firm muscle texture. Drying also takes longer because the relatively high fat content in the fillets will inhibit the movement of moisture to the surface of the flesh.

Lay the fillets on metal mesh trays or suspend them by the collarbone and place in the kiln cabinet. Again, if the kiln is fitted with an exhaust fan, drying can be effected with the fan in operation and the air entry shutter open. Ideally the relative humidity of the drying air should be between 60 and 70 per cent, with an air temperature of 18° to 24°C (65° to 75°F). If the humidity is much below 60 per cent, surface drying will progress too rapidly, inhibiting the escape of inner moisture; if above 70 per cent, drying will be too slow.

Dry the fillets as described or in an open, screened-in area, until a weight loss approaching 10 per cent is obtained. The time required will depend not only on the relative humidity of the drying air but also on the volume of air passing over the fillets and on the size of the fillets. To obtain the required weight loss could take up to 12 hours or longer.

3. Cold smoking. Begin smoking immediately after the drying period, using the same procedure as described in method one. The length of time spent smoke curing (see timetable) depends on the intensity of the smoke flavour preferred, but 8 hours is the minimum time.

4. Storing. At the conclusion of smoke processing, refrigerate the fillets if they are to be used within 7 to 10 days. If longer storage is required, wrap the fillets individually in freezer paper and freeze. Frozen smoked fillets may be stored for 3 to 4 weeks.

5. Serving. Salmon smoked by this method results in a product known as lox. It is very rich and should be sliced paper thin, across the grain. Traditionally it is served with cream cheese, rye or pumpernickel bread, capers and a wedge of lemon.

HOME PICKLING OF HERRING

There are two methods of pickling herring in the home. One is for short-term storage; the other involves canning for long-term storage.

Split herring lengthwise by cutting through rib bones on one side of backbone with a sharp knife.

Cut through bones, but not skin, and press sides flat butterfly style.

METHOD ONE (SHORT-TERM STORAGE)

Use strictly fresh herring, as soon after it is caught as possible, or salt (brine-cured) herring which has been soaked overnight in fresh water. Remove scales, head and viscera. Clean thoroughly and rinse well in cold fresh water.

Be sure to remove all traces of blood. Split herring lengthwise by cutting through rib bones on one side of the backbone with a sharp boning or paring knife, as shown in the drawing. Cut through bones but not skin, then press sides flat butterfly style.

1. Brining. Place herring in a brine solution of 315 g (1¼ cups) pickling salt to 1 L (1 qt.) water. (This quantity is for 12 herring.) Keep the herring submerged in the brine by using weights, and cure for 6 days in the refrigerator. Remove from brine and soak in cold fresh water for 20 to 30 minutes.

2. Packing in jars. Fillet the fish with a sharp knife. If the fillets are large, split them lengthwise. Pack the fillets in 228 mL (½ pt.) or 455 mL (1 pt.) jars. Pack each jar with a thin slice of onion, a bay leaf, and 2 mL (½ tsp.) of whole allspice berries.

3. Pickling. Make a vinegar solution in the following proportions:

185 mL	white vinegar	¾ cup
125 mL	water	½ cup
15 mL	sugar	1 Tbsp.

Bring vinegar solution to a boil and pour into jars to cover fillets. Cover the jars, cool and store in the refrigerator for 4 to 6 days for seasonings and vinegar solution to penetrate.

4. Storing. Since this herring is not pressure processed, it must be stored in the refrigerator at all times. Do not attempt to store for more than 3 weeks.

METHOD TWO (LONG-TERM STORAGE)

Read the general rules in the section on home canning before proceeding, as this method involves processing the fish under pressure.

Use strictly fresh herring. Scrape off scales, gut, remove fins, head and tail, but leave backbone in. Wash fish thoroughly and cut into jar-length pieces.

1. Brining. Soak fish in a brine of 250 g (1 cup) pickling salt to 4.5 L (1 gal.) water for one hour. Drain fish for 10 minutes.

2. Pickling. Prepare spiced vinegar sauce in the following proportions:

2 L	distilled white vinegar	2 qts.
50 mL	sugar	4 Tbsp.
1 L	water	1 qt.
1 mL	whole black peppercorns	¼ tsp.
1 mL	mustard seed	¼ tsp.
2 mL	whole cloves	½ tsp.
0.5 mL	cracked cardamom seed	⅛ tsp.
0.5 mL	ginger powder	⅛ tsp.
0.5 mL	bay leaves	⅛ tsp.

Add sugar and water to the vinegar. Add spices, tied loosely in a cheesecloth.

Cover and simmer for 60 minutes. Strain and use clear liquid. This amount is sufficient for about 2.7 kg (6 lbs.) herring. Divide liquid into ⅓ and ⅔.

3. Packing in jars. Sterilize jars (see directions given in step 1 under processing salmon or trout for home canning). Pack fish rather loosely into 228 mL (½ pt./8 oz.) or 455 mL (1 pt./16 oz.) jars. Dilute ⅓ of the full-strengh spiced vinegar sauce by mixing with an equal amount of water. Fill the jars with this diluted solution.

Place jars in a large pot with cold water up to a level of 5 cm (2″) below rims and bring to a boil. Boil 20 minutes. Invert jars over a wire screen and drain well.

In each jar, place a slice of raw onion, a bay leaf, 5 mL (1 tsp.) mixed pickling spices. Then fill the jars with remaining full-strength spiced vinegar sauce.

4. Pressure processing. Process in a pressure canner following your canner's directions accurately, at 10 lbs. (70 kPa) pressure, 116°C (240°F) for 90 minutes.

5. Check closure seals. See step 8 under processing salmon and trout in the section on home canning.

6. Storing. Processed jars of fish may be kept up to one year in a cool, dark place.

HOMEMADE CAVIAR

Homemade caviar may be made from the roe of any fish (except certain species of puffer fish) that lives in either salt or fresh water. (See fish roe under species for those whose roe is commonly used.) Immediately the fish is killed, the unbroken membrane (skein) of eggs must be removed. Keep it whole and cold until ready to prepare. Preparation should take place as soon as possible, since roe deteriorates quickly. Do not mix roe from different species and do not use frozen roe to make caviar.

Rinse the roe gently in cold running water to remove any blood or slime.

Then use your fingers to pop out carefully the individual eggs from the skein into a measuring cup. Prepare a brine solution in a separate container. For each 250 to 500 mL (1 to 2 cups) of eggs, stir 125 mL (½ cup) salt into 500 mL (2 cups) water. Pour eggs into brine and swirl briefly and gently. Leave eggs in brine for 2 to 3 hours to firm up and absorb some of the salt. Any remaining membrane will turn white; remove and discard. Drain eggs in a strainer, then immerse the strainer with eggs in a large bowl of fresh cold water, moving gently to rinse. Drain. Store in sterilized canning jars or equivalent in the refrigerator for 2 to 3 days for the salt to penetrate. The caviar is then ready to eat and at this time has a mild flavour.

The length of storage time dictates the strength of the caviar; individual taste varies considerably. Caviar stored for too long will begin to develop a yeasty or rancid flavour due to the growth of yeasts and molds in the product.

When this flavour is detected, dispose of the caviar, since it is no longer suitable for consumption. Homemade caviar may be stored refrigerated up to a maximum of 3 to 4 months.

Caviar makes exotic canapes and other hors d'oeuvre. For traditional serving methods, see whitefish caviar in recipe section.

✥NUTRITION✥

NUTRITIONAL VALUES

A vast variety of fish and shellfish is available fresh, frozen or canned. They are easy to prepare and quick to cook. Whether baked, broiled, poached, steamed, fried or barbecued, whether made into a soup, sandwich, hors d'oeuvre or main entrée, fish provides excitement to any menu and, in addition, is good for you. Nutritionally, the flesh of fish and all seafood as a source of protein is a completely satisfactory alternative to meat. The protein and fat in fish supply necessary energy, growth and maintenance, as well as many essential vitamins and minerals. The value of fish and shellfish as a delicious, satisfying and nutritious food has gone unrecognized for too long.

Fish and shellfish make a most important contribution to the daily diet, being a source of readily digestible protein of high nutritive value. Food proteins are made up of substances known as amino acids; over 20 of these amino acids have been identified, 10 of which are considered essential for the growth, maintenance and repair of body tissue. The ability of a source of protein to supply essential amino acids is a measure of its value in the diet. Fish not only provides us with all of the essential amino acids but has one added advantage; it contains much smaller amounts of connective tissue than red meats. This makes it more easily digested, so it is a natural choice for the diets of the elderly or very young, as well as anyone with digestive problems.

The fat content of fish varies widely from one species to another and from one season to another within the same species. Salmon and herring can contain up to 15 per cent body fat, while lingcod is usually less than one per cent fat. Although small amounts of certain fatty acids are required in the diet, fat as such is not essential for growth. Nevertheless, since fat is a better source of energy per unit of weight than either protein or carbohydrates, and since fat contributes much to the flavour of foods, it is usually thought to be a desirable component of the diet. Fatty acids obtainable from fish are very highly unsaturated, and since the content of fat in fish is generally low compared to most other protein-rich foods, it is considered an excellent food for anyone wishing to lose weight.

Lean saltwater fish from the Atlantic and Pacific include cod, cusk, flounder, haddock, hake, halibut, lingcod, pollock (Boston bluefish), redfish or ocean perch, rockfish, smelt and sole. *Fat saltwater fish* from the Atlantic and Pacific include sablefish or Alaska black cod, eel, herring, mackerel, salmon, tuna and turbot. *Lean freshwater fish* include carp, mullet, yellow perch, pickerel or walleye, northern pike, sauger, rainbow smelt and tullibee. *Fat freshwater fish* include arctic charr, goldeye, lake trout and lake whitefish.

Only very insignificant amounts of carbohydrates are present in fish, another reason why fish is excellent for those on a weight-reduction programme. Although carbohydrates are necessary—in small amounts—to provide the body with energy, foods high in carbohydrates are often high in calories.

People can obtain many of their normal vitamin requirements from marine vertebrates and invertebrates. Vitamin A, which is necessary for normal growth, good vision and resistance to infection, is present in small amounts in canned salmon. Several of the more oily types of canned fish (tuna, salmon, sardines and mackerel) are good sources of vitamin D, which aids in the proper use of calcium and phosphorus by the body for the development of strong bones and teeth. Both vitamin B12 and vitamin C are present in small amounts in fish flesh. Oysters, and the milts and roes of fish, are excellent sources of vitamin C, necessary for the maintenance of healthy teeth, gums and blood vessels. Small amounts of some of the B group of water-soluble vitamins—important for normal growth and development, especially the maintenance of nervous and digestive systems—are present in shellfish and fish livers and roe. The flesh of fresh fish contains adequate amounts of nicotinic acid and moderate quantities of pyridoxine, though it is deficient in thiamine, riboflavin and biotin. Folic acid occurs in significant amounts in raw fish but is largely destroyed by cooking and canning.

Fish are of particular interest in that they are usually good sources of iodine and copper. Iodine is necessary for the normal action of the thyroid gland, a deficiency of which produces goitre. Copper, like iron, is essential for the formation of haemoglobin, the protein that transports oxygen and carbon dioxide in the blood. Fluorine is also present in adequate quantities. For example, 112 g (4 oz.) of canned salmon containing the soft edible bones, if eaten every day, would provide the amount of fluorine necessary to prevent tooth decay in a growing child. Canned fish, in which the bones are retained and consumed, are a much better source of essential mineral elements than fresh or frozen fish. A normal serving of 112 g (4 oz.) of canned fish (with the exception of tuna, which is canned after the bones are removed) supplies 28 to 54 per cent of the daily calcium requirement, 24 to 44 per cent of the phosphorus, and 7 to 44 per cent of the iron (which prevents nutritional anemia). Although many people assume that fish caught in salt water contains more sodium than other foods, the reverse is true; fish from the sea contains no more sodium and in some cases appreciably less than is found in beef, pork or lamb and is, therefore, good for those on a low-salt diet.

NUTRITION CHART

The nutrients of many fish will vary, especially the fat content, depending on the area in which they are caught and the time of year. This nutrition chart gives a fair indication of the approximate nutritive values of most species of Atlantic, Pacific and fresh-water fish and shellfish commonly available on the commercial market. Some species are not included because figures are not available.

In the chart, nutritive values given are per 100 g (3.6 oz.). Dashes indicate lack of reliable data for a constituent believed to be present in a measurable amount. Note that the average cooked portion column of the chart indicates the calorie count and weight of average cooked or canned portions. Fried fish and shellfish have been dipped in egg, milk and bread-crumbs. All other cooked fish and shellfish are broiled unless marked otherwise.

For canned fish and shellfish, all vitamin values are based on drained solids.

NUTRITION CHART

TYPE OF FISH OR SHELLFISH	MOISTURE %	FOOD ENERGY kcal	PROTEIN g	CARBOHYDRATE g	FAT g	ASH g	CALCIUM mg	PHOSPHORUS mg
Abalone, raw	75.8	98	18.7	3.4	0.5	1.6	37	191
Alewife, raw	74.4	127	19.4	0	4.9	1.5	—	218
Arctic charr, frozen	71.0	134	20.8	0	5.2	—	36	56
Arctic charr, canned	64.2	176	25.6	0	8.2	—	149	368
Boston bluefish. See Pollock								
Capelin, raw	79.0	98	18.6	0	2.1	1.1	—	272
Caviar (sturgeon)	46.0	264	27.0	3.2	15.4	—	278	360
Cisco. See Tullibee								
Clams, raw (meat & liquid)	85.0	54	8.6	2.0	1.0	2.6	—	208
Clams, canned (meat & liquid)	86.3	52	7.9	2.8	0.7	2.3	55	137
Cod, raw	81.2	78	17.6	0	0.3	1.2	10	194
Cod, dried, salted	52.4	130	29.0	0	0.7	19.7	225	—
Cod, fish cakes, frozen	52.9	270	9.2	17.2	17.9	2.8	—	—
Crab, fresh, cooked	78.5	93	17.3	0.5	1.9	1.8	43	175
Crab, canned (meat only)	77.2	101	17.4	1.1	2.5	1.8	45	182
Cusk, raw	81.3	75	17.2	0	0.2	0.9	—	—
Dogfish, raw	72.3	156	17.6	0	9.0	1.0	—	—
Eel, raw	64.6	233	15.9	0	18.3	1.0	18	202
Eel, smoked	50.2	330	18.6	0	27.8	2.4	—	—
Fish sticks, breaded, frozen	65.8	176	16.6	6.5	8.9	2.2	11	167
Flounder (all flatfish)	81.3	79	16.7	0	0.8	1.2	12	195
Haddock, raw	80.5	79	18.3	0	0.1	1.4	23	197
Haddock, smoked	72.6	103	23.2	0	0.4	3.1	—	—
Hake, raw	81.8	74	16.5	0	0.4	1.3	41	142
Halibut, raw	76.5	100	20.9	0	1.2	1.4	13	211
Herring, raw (Atlantic)	69.0	176	17.3	0	11.3	2.1	—	256
Herring, raw (Pacific)	79.4	98	17.5	0	6.6	1.2	—	225
Herring, pickled	59.4	223	20.4	0	15.1	4.0	—	—
Herring, kippered	61.0	211	22.2	0	12.9	4.0	66	254
Herring, canned, plain	62.9	208	19.9	0	13.6	3.7	147	297
Inconnu, raw	72.0	146	19.9	0	6.8	1.3	—	—
Lake trout. See Trout								
Lake whitefish. See Whitefish								
Lobster, raw (whole)	78.5	91	16.9	0.5	1.9	2.2	29	183
Lobster, canned or cooked	76.8	95	18.7	0.3	1.5	2.7	65	192
Mackerel, raw (Atlantic)	67.2	191	19.0	0	12.2	1.6	5	239
Mackerel, raw (Pacific)	69.8	159	21.9	0	9.3	1.4	8	274
Mackerel, canned (liquid & solids)	66.0	183	19.3	0	11.1	3.2	185	274
Mussels, raw (meat only)	78.6	95	14.4	3.3	2.2	1.5	88	236
Northern pike, raw	80.0	88	18.3	0	1.1	1.1	—	—
Ocean perch (Atlantic). See Redfish								
Ocean perch, raw	79.0	95	19.0	0	1.5	1.1	—	—
Ocean perch, fried	59.0	227	19.0	6.8	13.3	1.9	33	226

IRON mg	SODIUM mg	POTASSIUM mg	VITAMIN A IU	THIAMINE mg	RIBOFLAVIN mg	NIACIN mg	VITAMIN C mg	AVERAGE COOKED PORTION		
								Total Calories	MEASURE	Wt. in oz.
2.4	—	—	—	0.18	0.14	—	—	88	90 g	3
—	—	—	—	—	—	—	—	114	90 g fillet	3
8.2	—	—	—	0.13	0.58	3.2	1.0	150	112 g fillet	4
—	—	—	—	0.09	0.83	4.5	—	158	90 g	3
0.4	—	—	—	0.01	0.12	1.4	—	88	90 g (6 fish)	3
11.8	2228	182	—	—	—	—	—	42	16 g	0.5
—	—	—	—	—	—	—	—	92	112 g	4
4.1	—	140	—	0.01	0.11	1.0	—	88	90 g (drained)	3
0.4	70[1]	382	—	0.06	0.07	2.2	2	85	112 g fillet	4
—	—	—	—	—	—	—	—	120	90 g fillet	3
—	—	—	—	—	—	—	—	270	100 g (1 fishcake)	3.5
0.8	—	—	2170	0.16	0.08	2.8	2	90	86 g	3
0.8	1000[1]	110	—	0.08	0.08	1.9	—	90	86 g	3
—	—	—	—	0.03	0.08	2.3	—	84	112 g fillet	4
—	—	—	—	0.05	—	—	—	156	100 g fillet	3.5
0.7	—	—	1610	0.22	0.36	1.4	—	210	90 g	3
—	—	—	—	—	—	—	—	297	90 g	3
0.4	475	208	0	0.04	0.07	1.6	—	170	90 g (3 sticks)	3
0.8	78	342	—	0.05	0.05	1.7	—	88	112 g fillet	4
0.7	61	304	—	0.04	0.07	3.0	—	188	112 g fillet (fried)	4
—	—	—	—	0.06	0.05	2.1	—	92	90 g fillet	3
—	74	363	—	0.10	0.20	—	—	84	112 g fillet (steamed)	4
0.7	54[2]	449	440	0.07	0.07	8.3	—	145	112 g fillet	4
1.1	—	—	110	0.02	0.15	3.6	—	197	112 g fish	4
1.3	74	420	100	0.02	0.16	3.5	3	120	100 g fish	3
—	—	—	—	—	—	—	—	112	50 g fillet	1.5
1.4	—	—	30	—	0.28	3.3	—	211	100 g fish	3.5
1.8	—	—	—	—	0.18	—	—	884	425 g can	15
—	—	—	—	—	—	—	—	166	112 g fillet	4
0.6	—	—	—	0.40	0.05	1.5	—	138	145 g meat	5
0.8	210	180	—	0.10	0.07	—	—	485	250 g lobster Newburg	8
1.0	—	—	(450)	0.15	0.33	8.2	—	248	105 g fillet (fried)	3.5
2.1	—	—	120	—	—	—	—	204	112 g fillet	4
2.1	—	—	430	0.06	0.21	5.8	—	765	425 g can	15
3.4	289	315	—	0.16	0.21	—	—	85	90 g (meat only)	3
—	—	—	—	—	—	—	—	99	112 g fillet	4
—	63	390	—	—	—	—	—	95	105 g (steamed)	3.5
1.3	153	284	—	0.10	0.11	1.8	—	227	105 g fillet	3.5

NUTRITION CHART

TYPE OF FISH OR SHELLFISH	MOISTURE %	FOOD ENERGY kcal	PROTEIN g	CARBOHYDRATE g	FAT g	ASH g	CALCIUM mg	PHOSPHORUS mg
Octopus	82.2	73	15.3	0	0.8	1.5	29	173
Oysters, raw (Atlantic)	84.6	46	8.4	3.4	1.8	—	94	143
Oysters, raw (Pacific)	79.1	91	10.6	6.4	2.2	1.7	85	153
Oysters, fried	54.7	239	8.6	18.6	13.9	1.5	152	241
Oysters, canned (solids & liquid)	82.2	76	8.5	4.9	2.2	2.2	28	124
Pickerel, raw	78.3	93	19.3	0	1.2	1.2	—	214
Pollock	77.4	95	20.4	0	0.9	1.3	—	—
Redfish, raw	79.7	88	18.0	0	1.2	1.1	20	207
Sablefish	71.6	190	13.0	0	14.9	1.0	—	—
Salmon, fresh (broiled or baked)	63.4	182	27.0	0	12.4	1.6	—	414
Salmon, smoked	58.9	176	21.6	0	9.3	—	14	245
Sockeye, canned (solids & liquid)	67.2	171	20.3	0	9.3	2.7	259[3]	344
Coho, canned (solids & liquid)	69.3	153	20.8	0	7.1	2.4	244[3]	288
Pink, canned (solids & liquid)	70.8	141	20.5	0	5.9	2.3	196[3]	286
Sardines, canned in oil (solids only)	57.4	214	25.7	1.2	11.0	4.7	386	586
Sauger	80.8	84	17.9	0	0.8	1.1	—	—
Scallops, raw	80.3	78	14.8	3.4	0.1	1.4	26	208
Shad, raw	70.4	170	18.6	0	10.0	1.3	20	260
Shrimp, raw	70.0	91	18.0	2.0	1.0	1.4	63	—
Shrimp, french-fried (batter)	56.9	225	20.3	10.0	10.8	2.0	72	191
Shrimp, canned (solids only)	66.2	127	26.8	—	1.4	5.8	115	263
Skate, raw	77.8	98	21.5	0	0.7	1.2	—	—
Smelt, raw	79.6	118	14.6	0	6.2	1.2	—	—
Sole. See Flounder								
Squid, raw	80.2	84	16.4	1.5	0.9	1.0	12	119
Swordfish, raw	75.9	118	19.2	0	4.0	1.3	19	195
Trout, raw	73.1	144	19.9	0	6.5	1.2	—	—
Trout, frozen	70.6	168	18.3	0	10.0	—	—	238
Trout, canned	59.6	220	23.1	0	14.1	—	52	47
Tullibee	79.7	96	17.7	0	2.3	1.1	12	206
Tuna, fresh (bluefin), raw	70.5	145	25.2	0	8.1	1.3	—	—
Tuna, canned in broth & oil (solids & liquid)	61.3	207	26.1	0	10.6	1.8	11	242
Turbot, raw	74.5	146	16.4	0	8.4	1.0	—	210
Whitefish, raw	71.7	155	18.9	0	8.2	1.2	—	270
Yellow perch, raw	79.2	91	19.5	0	0.9	1.2	—	180

NOTES
1. If dipped or rinsed in brine, value is about 225 mg per 100 g.
2. Two frozen samples dipped in brine contained 360 mg of sodium per 100 g.
3. Values apply only if bones are eaten.
4. Includes salt added to canned salmon.

IRON mg	SODIUM mg	POTASSIUM mg	VITAMIN A IU	THIAMINE mg	RIBOFLAVIN mg	NIACIN mg	VITAMIN C mg	AVERAGE COOKED PORTION		
								Total Calories	MEASURE	Wt. in oz.
—	—	—	—	0.02	0.06	1.8	—	66	90 g	3
5.5	73	121	310	0.14	0.18	2.5	—	19	28 g (2 medium)	1
7.2	—	—	—	0.12	—	1.3	30	200	238 g (13-19 medium)	8
8.1	206	203	440	0.17	0.29	3.2	—	108	45 g (4 medium)	1.5
5.6	—	70	—	0.02	0.20	0.8	—	224	340 g can	12
0.4	51	319	—	0.25	0.16	2.3	—	105	112 g fillet	4
—	48	350	—	0.05	0.10	1.6	—	178	112 g fillet (w. butter)	4
1.0	79	269	—	0.10	0.08	1.9	—	288	90 g fillet (fried)	3
—	56	358	—	0.11	0.09	—	—	190	100 g	3.5
1.2	116	443	160	0.16	0.06	9.8	—	192	90 g fillet	3
—	—	—	—	—	—	—	—	158	90 g	3
1.2	522[4]	344	230	0.04	0.16	7.3	—	154	90 g	3
0.9	351[4]	339	80	0.03	0.18	7.4	—	138	90 g	3
0.8	387[4]	361	70	0.03	0.18	8.0	—	127	90 g	3
2.7	510	560	220	0.02	0.17	4.8	—	182	90 g (drained)	3
—	—	—	—	—	—	—	—	90	112 g fillet	4
1.8	150	420	0	0.04	0.10	1.4	—	90	112 g	4
0.5	54	330	—	0.15	0.24	8.4	—	228	112 g (baked w. bacon)	4
1.6	140	220	—	0.02	0.03	6.3	—	91	100 g (20 small)	3.5
2.0	186	229	—	0.04	0.08	2.7	—	203	90 g (6 large)	3
3.1	140	220	60	0.01	0.03	2.2	—	110	90 g (drained)	3
—	—	—	—	0.02	—	—	—	110	112 g (steamed)	4
—	—	—	—	0.04	0.04	—	—	88	90 g (6 fish)	3
0.5	—	—	—	0.02	0.12	—	—	94	112 g	4
0.9	—	—	1580	0.05	0.05	8.0	—	237	145 g	5.5
—	—	—	—	0.06	0.06	—	—	194	90 g fish	3
0.8	—	—	—	0.09	0.12	2.7	—	—	—	—
12.3	—	—	—	0.12	0.28	1.8	—	198	90 g	3
0.5	47	319	—	0.09	0.10	3.3	—	120	100 g fish	3.5
1.3	—	—	—	—	—	—	—	175	112 g (baked)	4
1.3	800	280	87	0.04	0.10	11.7	—	177	90 g (drained)	3
—	—	—	—	0.01	—	—	—	187	90 g fillet	3
0.4	52	299	2260	0.14	0.12	3.0	—	174	112 g fillet	4
0.6	68	230	—	0.06	0.17	1.7	—	230	250 g fish	8

SOURCES

U.S. Department of Agriculture, *Handbook No. 8* (1969).

U.S. Department of Agriculture, *Handbook No. 456* (1975).

Canada, Ministry of National Health and Welfare, *Nutrient Values of Some Common Foods* (revised, 1979).

Canada, Fisheries Development Branch, *Guide to the Handling and Preparing of Freshwater Fish* (1983) by D. G. Iredale and R. K. York of the Freshwater Institute, Department of Fisheries and Oceans.

3

BASIC
FISH
COOKERY

TIMING RULE

COOKING METHODS:
Baking
Broiling
Pan Frying
Deep Frying
Poaching or Steaming
Barbecuing

✤Timing Rule✤

Although flavour, texture and thickness vary quite considerably among the different species, it should be emphasized very strongly that the timing rule for cooking fish applies to all species. Note also that most white-fleshed fish are interchangeable in practically any recipe.

Because fish contains very little connective tissue, it does not need long slow cooking—in fact, overcooked fish is dry and tasteless. Use a high temperature and follow the timing rule, and your fish will retain its flavour and be moist and succulent. Fish should be cooked only until its translucent flesh becomes opaque. An easy way to test this is to part the flakes with a fork; if the flesh is milky and opaque all through the thickest part, it is done.

To cook fresh fish by practically any method, use the timing rule of 5 to 7 minutes per centimetre (10 to 12 minutes per inch) of thickness, measured through the thickest part.

To cook partially thawed fish, add 1 to 2 minutes to the timing rule. The common belief that fish should be cooked from the frozen state is incorrect. Frozen fish is best when partially thawed so that it is flexible but still retains ice crystals. If fish becomes totally thawed and limp, much of its natural juices will be lost, resulting in dry, tough flesh. To help retain these juices, dip partially or completely thawed fillets or steaks into a bath of lemon juice and then dip in seasoned flour before using any recipe. Keep a brown paper or plastic bag of seasoned flour for this purpose if you eat fish often.

To cook solidly frozen fish, double the time specified in the timing rule: that is, cook 10 to 14 minutes per centimetre (20 to 24 minutes per inch) of thickness. Cooking solidly frozen fish is a practice to be avoided, as common sense will tell you that when using a high heat of 230°C (450°F), the outside will be overcooked, tough and dried out before the heat can penetrate through to the centre.

✍COOKING METHODS✍

There are seven basic methods of cooking fish:

in the oven by baking or broiling
in the frying pan by pan frying
in deep fat by deep frying
in or over liquid by poaching or steaming
over hot coals by barbecuing

With each of these cooking methods, it is important to control the time and temperature of cooking.

BAKING

Baking is excellent for whole stuffed fish, thick fillets or steaks, and seafood casseroles.

Preheat the oven to 230°C (450°F). At this temperature, the cooking time will be very short. The timing rule applies whether for a thin fillet or a whole stuffed fish. When the fish is cooked under a blanket of sauce, add 5 minutes per 2.5 cm (1″) of thickness to the timing rule. If fish is cooked in cream or sauces containing eggs or cheese, a moderate oven temperature of 180°C (350°F) should be used to prevent separation or toughening of these proteins, and the time given in the recipe should be followed.

BROILING

Broiling is excellent for fillets, steaks, fish sticks and individual ramekin dishes such as Coquilles St. Jacques (see index). It is also an easy and quick way of producing a variety of fish dishes just by placing different toppings on the fish prior to cooking.

Preheat the broiler. Arrange the fish on a well-greased broiler pan; baste with melted butter or margarine and season to taste or put on your chosen topping. Place the fish 7 to 10 cm (3 to 4″) below the broiler unit, leaving the oven door slightly open according to manufacturer's instructions. Use the timing rule, turning once halfway through cooking; season and baste the second side. Thin pieces less than 2.5 cm (1″) need not be turned.

PAN FRYING

Pan frying is suitable for steaks, fillets and small whole fish. It is important to have enough fat to cover the bottom of the pan, about 3 mm (⅛″), and to have it very hot but not smoking before frying the fish. Use a fat with a high smoking temperature (meaning one that will reach a high temperature before smoking) for best results. Cut the fish into serving-size portions and coat with seasoned flour or dip into seasoned milk (or beaten egg) and roll in one of a variety of coatings such as breadcrumbs (see breadings and batters in recipe section). Follow the timing rule but turn the fish once in the middle of cooking. Both sides should be a golden brown.

DEEP FRYING

Fillets, smelt, fish cakes and shellfish are excellent when fried in deep fat. The choice of cooking fat is most important for this method. Fats with a high smoking temperature (see pan frying) are best and will minimize cooking odours. These fats are also less readily absorbed by the food than those with a low smoking temperature. Most vegetable oils are ideal.

Preheat fat to a temperature of 190°C (375°F). Cut up fish into pieces of uniform size and a thickness of about 1.25 cm (½″). Bread or dip fish into batter (see breadings and batters in recipe section), then fry until golden brown. Drain excess fat by placing the fried fish on paper towelling before serving. Before frying additional portions, the temperature of the fat should be returned to 190°C (375°F). After use, fat may be clarified by frying a piece of raw potato in it and straining through a cheesecloth.

POACHING OR STEAMING

Poaching or steaming is ideal for smoked fish, fillets, steaks and portions of fresh or frozen fish which are to be cooked for use in salads, casseroles, fish cakes or creamed dishes. As a measure, 500 g (1 lb.) of fish fillets, when cooked, make 500 mL (2 cups) of flaked fish.

To poach fish, bring to a boil enough water just to cover the fish and add about 2 mL (½ tsp.) salt. Immerse the fish and bring to a boil again, then reduce heat and simmer gently; follow the timing rule. Whole fish, thick fillets, steaks or chunks may also be poached in a court bouillon (see court bouillons in recipe section), using a similar method.

Fish may also be poached in the oven, enclosed in a sheet of aluminum foil. This method helps to retain moisture. The fish will cook in its own natural juices, to which lemon juice or white wine, butter and seasonings may be added. Apply the timing rule but allow 5 additional minutes to allow heat to penetrate the foil.

Smoked fish may be poached in milk or water (milk is richer), either in a shallow pan on top of the stove or in a casserole in the oven. The milk may be saved and used to make a sauce to pour over the fish (see recipe for fish poached in milk).

To steam fish, place in a perforated steamer tray over lightly boiling water. Cover pot with a tightly fitting lid and steam for slightly longer than the timing rule.

BARBECUING

Barbecuing is one of the most popular methods of cooking fish and seafood in the summer, and many people who have the facilities also barbecue throughout the winter. The preparation is easy, the cooking quick, and the results are deliciously different.

If the fish or seafood is frozen, thaw it to refrigerator temperature before barbecuing to ensure even cooking throughout. A whole fish should be scaled prior to barbecuing. Fish flesh has little connective tissue and breaks up easily when cooked, so a separate hinged grill or a chicken wire envelope should be used to avoid losing the fish through the barbecue grill. To prevent fish from sticking to the barbecue, oil the grill, chicken wire and fish well before cooking. Keep a pastry brush and separate jar of oil on hand for this purpose.

Light the coals 20 minutes before using the barbecue. They should be grey before you start cooking. Place the fish 7 to 10 cm (3 to 4″) above the coals.

Since there are many variables attached to the timing of barbecuing such as the heat of the coals, the distance of food from the coals, the temperature of the food and the weather, it is impossible to give set rules. However, the barbecuing timetable will be of assistance in achieving the best results.

BARBECUING TIMETABLE

SIZE OF FISH	APPROXIMATE TIME (minutes)	COMMENTS
Whole fish, small	12 to 18	Turn once, mid-way
Whole fish, large	30 to 60	Turn once, mid-way
Split fish, small	8 to 12	No need to turn
Split fish, large	20 to 40	Turn if thicker than 2.5 cm (1″)
Fillets	8 to 18	Turn if thicker than 2.5 cm (1″)
Steaks, 2.5 cm (1″) thick	6 to 9	Turn once, mid-way
Steaks, 2.5 to 4 cm (1 to 1½″) thick	8 to 12	Turn once, mid-way
Steaks, 5 cm (2″) thick	10 to 18	Turn once, mid-way

4

RECIPES

HORS D'OEUVRE AND APPETIZERS
SOUPS AND CHOWDERS
SALADS
LIGHT ENTREES
MAIN COURSE ENTREES
SANDWICHES
MARINADES
COURT BOUILLONS
BREADINGS AND BATTERS
STUFFINGS
SAUCES
SALAD DRESSINGS

HORS D'OEUVRE AND ᔥAPPETIZERSᔥ

ANCHOVY-STUFFED EGGS

56-g can	anchovy fillets	2-oz. can
12	hard-cooked eggs	12
50 mL	mayonnaise	¼ cup
50 mL	sour cream	¼ cup
15 mL	medium-dry sherry	1 Tbsp.
15 mL	parsley	1 Tbsp.
1 mL	orégano	¼ tsp.
1 mL	salt	¼ tsp.
0.5 mL	white pepper	⅛ tsp.

Drain anchovy fillets well and mash, reserving 24 small pieces for garnish.

Cut eggs in half lengthwise and carefully remove yolks. Mash yolks with mayonnaise, sour cream, sherry and anchovies. Mix in parsley, orégano, salt and pepper. Spoon or pipe the yolk mixture back into the whites. Place a small piece of anchovy on top of each egg half and garnish with parsley. Makes 24 egg halves.

CLAM AND CHEESE DIP

125 g	shelled cooked clams OR	4 oz.
128-g can	minced clams	4.5-oz. can
250-g pkg.	cream cheese	8-oz. pkg.
50 mL	mayonnaise	¼ cup
10 mL	lemon juice	2 tsp.
15 mL	onion, finely chopped	1 Tbsp.
2 mL	salt	½ tsp.
1 mL	pepper	¼ tsp.
3 mL	fresh dill, chopped OR	¾ tsp.
1 mL	dried dill weed	¼ tsp.

Drain clams and reserve liquid. If using fresh clams, mince. Beat cream cheese with mayonnaise, lemon juice, onion and seasonings. Gradually beat in a little reserved liquid until dipping consistency is reached. Stir in minced clams and refrigerate for one hour before serving. Makes about 375 mL (1½ cups).

CLAM TURNOVERS

250 g	shelled clams	8 oz.
	pastry, enough for a 2-crust pie	
50 mL	seafood cocktail sauce (see index)	¼ cup
1	egg, lightly beaten OR	1
50 mL	milk	¼ cup

Drain clams well and chop coarsely.

Roll pastry about 3 mm (⅛″) thick and cut into about 24 circles, 7.5 cm (3″) in diameter. On each circle, place 5 to 7 mL (1 to 1½ tsp.) clams and about 2 mL (½ tsp.) cocktail sauce.

Fold pastry over and wet edges with water to seal. Place on a lightly greased cookie sheet. Brush pastry with beaten egg (or milk) and prick with a fork to allow steam to escape.

Preheat oven to 220°C (425°F) and bake for 15 minutes or until pastry is lightly browned. Makes approximately 24 turnovers.

Options: oysters or crabmeat

CRAB BITES

175 g	fresh crab meat OR	6 oz.
170-g can	crab meat, drained and flaked	6-oz. can
15 mL	butter	1 Tbsp.
30 mL	flour	2 Tbsp.
1 mL	salt	¼ tsp.
0.5 mL	paprika	⅛ tsp.
75 mL	milk	⅓ cup
1 mL	Worcestershire sauce	¼ tsp.
5 mL	parsley, minced	1 tsp.
1	egg	1
30 mL	water	2 Tbsp.
175 mL	fine dry breadcrumbs, lightly seasoned	¾ cup
	oil for deep frying	

Melt butter in a saucepan, add flour, salt and paprika; stir until blended. Add milk gradually and cook over medium heat, stirring constantly, until smooth and thickened. Remove from heat, add Worcestershire, parsley and crab meat. Chill. Form mixture into small balls about 1.25 cm (½″) in diameter.

In a bowl, make an egg wash by beating egg slightly with water. Dip crab bites into breadcrumbs, then in egg wash, and again into breadcrumbs. Let stand for about 5 minutes to dry coating.

Preheat oil to 190°C (375°F), then deep fry crab bites for about one minute or until golden brown. Drain on absorbent paper. Makes about 30 crab bites.

Insert a toothpick in each crab bite. If desired, serve with a medium-hot dip such as seafood cocktail sauce (see index).

Options: fresh or canned shrimp, clams

CRAB-DILL CANAPES

250 g	crab meat	8 oz.
15 mL	dry white wine OR sherry	1 Tbsp.
15 mL	fresh dill, chopped OR	1 Tbsp.
5 mL	dried dill weed	1 tsp.
15 mL	butter	1 Tbsp.
15 mL	flour	1 Tbsp.
125 mL	light cream	½ cup
	salt and pepper	
8 or 9 slices	white bread	8 or 9 slices

Drain crab and remove any bits of shell or cartilage; break into chunks. Combine crab meat, wine and dill; set aside.

In a small pot, melt butter over low heat and blend in flour. Pour cream slowly into butter and flour mixture, stirring to blend. Turn heat up to medium and cook, stirring constantly, until thickened. Season to taste with salt and pepper. Fold sauce into crab mixture.

Cut 3 or 4 circles out of each slice of bread and toast on one side only under the broiler. Spread soft side generously with crab mixture. Just before serving, broil 1 or 2 minutes until lightly browned. Makes about 30 canapés.

Options: fresh or canned shrimp

DEEP-FRIED SCALLOPS WITH GUACAMOLE

1 kg	scallops	2 lbs.
	bag of seasoned flour	
	batter of your choice (see index)	
	oil for deep frying	

Coat scallops first in seasoned flour, then in batter. Preheat oil to 190°C (375°F) and deep fry scallops for 2 to 3 minutes. Drain on paper towels. Serve hot with guacamole dip. Serves 16 to 18 as an hors d'oeuvre.

GUACAMOLE DIP

1 large	avocado	1 large
1 small	tomato	1 small
15 mL	lemon juice	1 Tbsp.
1 clove	garlic, minced	1 clove
10 mL	onion, minced (Bermuda, if possible)	2 tsp.
15 mL	canned green chili peppers, minced	1 Tbsp.
2 mL	chili powder	½ tsp.
5 mL	salt	1 tsp.
dash	Tabasco sauce	dash

Peel, pit and mash avocado. Peel, seed and finely chop tomato. Combine all ingredients and mix thoroughly with a fork. Chill for one hour before serving.

Options: shrimp, lobster or squid. If using squid, clean, wash and cut into 1.25 cm (½″) rings, simmer for 10 minutes and drain before deep frying.

OYSTER PUFFS

250 g	shucked oysters with liquid OR	8 oz.
2 160-g cans	oysters	2 5-oz. cans
75 mL	butter	⅓ cup
4 mL	salt	¾ tsp.
175 mL	flour	¾ cup
3	eggs	3
	oil for deep frying	

If using shucked oysters, simmer in their liquid until edges begin to curl. Drain oysters (whether shucked or canned) and reserve 175 mL (¾ cup) liquid. Chop oysters coarsely and set aside.

In a saucepan, bring reserved liquid, butter and salt to boiling point. Add flour all at once and stir vigorously until mixture leaves sides of pan and forms a ball. Remove from heat and cool slightly. Add the eggs, one at a time, beating well after each addition. Stir in the oysters.

Preheat oil to 190°C (375°F). Drop batter by teaspoonfuls into the oil and deep fry for 7 to 10 minutes or until puffed and golden brown. Serve hot with seafood cocktail sauce (see index). Makes 35 to 40 puffs.

Options: clams or mussels

OYSTERS ON THE HALF SHELL

24	oysters in the shell	24
250 mL	seafood cocktail sauce (see index)	1 cup
6 wedges	lemon	6 wedges
6 sprigs	parsley	6 sprigs
	crushed ice	

Shuck and drain oysters; replace each oyster in the lower half of its shell. Put some crushed ice into six shallow bowls or soup plates. Place four half shells containing oysters on the ice in each bowl. Place 30 mL (2 Tbsp.) of seafood cocktail sauce in a small container in the centre of each bowl. Garnish each bowl with a lemon wedge and a sprig of parsley. Serves 6.

OYSTERS ROCKEFELLER

12	oysters in the shell	12
50 mL	butter	¼ cup
250 mL	spinach, minced	1 cup
50 mL	onion, finely chopped	¼ cup
30 mL	celery, finely chopped	2 Tbsp.
30 mL	parsley, minced	2 Tbsp.
50 mL	dried breadcrumbs	¼ cup
2 mL	salt	½ tsp.
15 mL	anise-flavoured liqueur	1 Tbsp.
dash	cayenne pepper OR Tabasco sauce	dash
2 slices	bacon, diced	2 slices
	rock salt	

Shuck and drain oysters; replace each oyster in the lower half of its shell.

In a saucepan, melt butter; add spinach, onion, celery and parsley, then cook for 6 minutes. Add breadcrumbs and seasonings, stirring to mix thoroughly.

Place half shells containing oysters on a bed of rock salt in a baking pan to keep them steady. Cover each oyster with spinach mixture, then top with diced bacon.

Preheat oven to 205°C (400°F) and bake for about 10 minutes until the bacon is crisp. Serves 6 as an appetizer.

OYSTER-STUFFED MUSHROOM CAPS

500 g	shucked oysters	1 pint
15 mL	butter, melted	1 Tbsp.
30 mL	medium-dry sherry	2 Tbsp.
0.5 mL	salt	⅛ tsp.
12	mushroom caps, large	12

Dip oysters in mixture of melted butter, sherry and salt. Place one oyster (or piece of oyster cut to size) in each mushroom cap. Place in a lightly greased baking pan; pour remaining butter and sherry mixture over the oysters and mushroom caps.

Preheat oven to 230°C (450°F) and bake for 10 minutes. Serve hot. Makes enough for 3 to 4 people.

Options: clams or mussels (use 2 or 3 to each mushroom cap, depending on size)

PICKLED CLAMS

500 g	shelled clams with liquid OR	1 lb.
3 140-g cans	clams	3 5-oz. cans
500 mL	vinegar	2 cups
1	bay leaf	1
7 mL	whole cloves	1½ tsp.
5 mL	whole peppercorns	1 tsp.
5 mL	cinnamon	1 tsp.
15 mL	salt	1 Tbsp.
10 mL	nutmeg	2 tsp.
10 mL	mustard seed	2 tsp.

Shell and drain clams, reserving liquid. To this liquid, add enough water to make 500 mL (2 cups).

In a large saucepan, combine liquid, vinegar and seasonings; simmer long enough (about 30 minutes) to blend spices. Strain. Add clams to strained liquid and bring to a boil. Set aside to cool.

These clams should be prepared the day before eating. Store in the refrigerator; they will keep well for 1 to 2 weeks.

Drain before serving. Good served on crackers or rye bread spread with cream cheese.

SALMON DIP

220-g can	sockeye OR coho	7.75-oz. can
375 mL	sour cream	1½ cups
125 mL	chili sauce	½ cup
50 mL	sweet pickle relish	¼ cup
125 mL	French dressing (see index) OR prepared French dressing	½ cup
5 mL	horseradish	1 tsp.
15 mL	lemon juice	1 Tbsp.
15 mL	chives, chopped	1 Tbsp.
2 drops	Tabasco sauce	2 drops
1 mL	salt	¼ tsp.

Blend all ingredients well and refrigerate for 2 to 4 hours. Makes 1 L (4 cups) of a delicious and nourishing dip to serve with raw vegetables such as cauliflower, carrot sticks, green onions, zucchini strips, celery, cherry tomatoes and radishes.

SEAFOOD COCKTAIL

375 g	shelled cooked shrimp, chopped	12 oz.
50 mL	ketchup	3 Tbsp.
50 mL	chili sauce	3 Tbsp.
15 mL	Worcestershire sauce	1 Tbsp.
30 mL	horseradish	2 Tbsp.
2 drops	Tabasco sauce	2 drops
10 mL	lemon juice	2 tsp.
	lettuce	
6 wedges	lemon	6 wedges
6 sprigs	parsley	6 sprigs

To make cocktail sauce, combine ketchup, chili sauce, Worcestershire, horseradish and Tabasco. Chill for at least one hour to blend the flavours.

Line six cocktail glasses with lettuce leaves. Fill each glass with shrimp and top with 30 mL (2 Tbsp.) of the cocktail sauce. Garnish with parsley and lemon wedges. Serves 6.

Options: crab, clams, oysters or fillets (cooked) of most white-fleshed fish. This seafood cocktail is also excellent served on avocado halves instead of lettuce.

SHRIMP-CHEESE BALL

125 g	shelled cooked shrimp OR	4 oz.
120-g can	shrimp	4.5-oz. can
250-g pkg.	cream cheese	8-oz. pkg.
250 mL	medium cheddar cheese, grated	1 cup
30 mL	medium-dry sherry	2 Tbsp.
5 mL	dry mustard	1 tsp.
5 mL	Worcestershire sauce	1 tsp.
50 mL	toasted sesame seeds	3 Tbsp.

If using canned shrimp, drain, rinse under cold running water, and drain again. Chop shrimp into small pieces.

Use an electric blender to beat cream cheese until soft. Add cheddar cheese and beat well.

In another bowl, combine sherry, dry mustard and Worcestershire, then mix all into cheese mixture. Beat in shrimp last. Shape the mixture into a ball, cover and refrigerate for 2 to 3 hours or until firm.

When ready to serve, reshape ball and roll in sesame seeds. Serve with crackers. Makes about 500 mL (2 cups).

SHRIMP-CHEESE DIP

125 g	shelled cooked shrimp OR	4 oz.
120-g can	shrimp	4.5-oz. can
250-g pkg.	cream cheese, softened	8-oz. pkg.
125 mL	mayonnaise	½ cup
30 mL	chili sauce	2 Tbsp.
50 mL	French dressing (see index) OR prepared French dressing	¼ cup
30 mL	green onion, finely chopped	2 Tbsp.

If using canned shrimp, drain, rinse under cold running water, and drain again. Chop shrimp into small pieces.

Blend cream cheese, mayonnaise, chili sauce, French dressing and green onion until smooth. Add shrimp and mix well. Chill several hours before serving. Makes 500 mL (2 cups). This is a tasty dip for fresh raw vegetables.

SHRIMP-STUFFED PEARS

125 g	shelled cooked shrimp OR	4 oz.
120-g can	shrimp	4.5-oz. can
6 to 7	pears OR	6 to 7
796-mL can	pear halves	28-oz. can
250-g pkg.	cream cheese, softened	8-oz. pkg.
15 mL	milk	1 Tbsp.
5 mL	lemon juice	1 tsp.
0.5 mL	salt	⅛ tsp.
5 mL	fresh dill, chopped OR	1 tsp.
0.5 mL	dried dill weed	⅛ tsp
	paprika	
	stuffed olives	
	lemon wedges	
	lettuce	

If using canned shrimp, drain, rinse under cold water, and drain again.

Peel, halve and core pears. If using canned pears, drain well.

Beat cream cheese with milk until smooth. Stir in shrimp, lemon juice, salt and dill. Fill the hollow of each pear half with shrimp mixture. Sprinkle with paprika and decorate with stuffed olives. Place in a lettuce cup with lemon wedges. Makes 6 to 7 servings of 2 pear halves per person.

Options: crab meat or lobster meat

SMELT PATE

250 g	smelt	8 oz.
2 250-g pkgs.	cream cheese	2 8-oz. pkgs.
5 mL	Worcestershire sauce	1 tsp.
10 mL	prepared mustard	2 tsp.
30 mL	lemon juice	2 Tbsp.
30 mL	onion, grated	2 Tbsp.
30 mL	chives, finely chopped	2 Tbsp.
125 mL	flaked almonds, crushed	½ cup

Steam the smelt for 7 to 10 minutes, cool, then bone and mash.

Beat the cream cheese until soft and add Worcestershire, mustard, lemon juice, onion and chives. Mix thoroughly, then add mashed smelt and beat until well blended. Shape into a mound on a serving plate and cover with flaked crushed almonds. Refrigerate for several hours before using. Serve with crackers. Makes approximately 750 mL (3 cups).

TUNA-STUFFED LOGS

184-g can	flaked tuna	6.5-oz. can
30 mL	mayonnaise	2 Tbsp.
6	stuffed olives, minced	6
1 mL	salt	¼ tsp.
1 mL	paprika	¼ tsp.
2 mL	horseradish	½ tsp.
16	celery sticks, 5 cm (2″) long	16
	stuffed olives, sliced	
	parsley sprigs	

Drain tuna well, then mix with mayonnaise, olives, salt, paprika and horseradish. Fill each celery stick with 15 mL (1 Tbsp.) of tuna mixture. Garnish with a slice of stuffed olive and a small sprig of parsley. Makes 16 logs.

Options: canned mackerel or salmon

TURBOT MORSELS

500 g	turbot fillets	1 lb.
375 mL	mashed potato	1½ cups
1	well-beaten egg	1
15 mL	melted butter	1 Tbsp.
3 mL	salt	¾ tsp.
1 mL	pepper	¼ tsp.
15 mL	green pepper, minced	1 Tbsp.
6 mL	horseradish	1½ tsp.
1 mL	dried fennel	¼ tsp.
	oil for deep frying	

Steam turbot over boiling water for 10 to 12 minutes or until cooked. Let cool and flake.

Mix mashed potato with beaten egg and melted butter. Add fish, salt, pepper, green pepper, horseradish and fennel, then beat until smooth. Shape lightly into small balls.

Preheat oil to 190°C (375°F) and deep fry for 2 to 3 minutes or until golden brown. Serves 4.

Options: cod, hake, pollock (Boston bluefish), cusk or pickerel

WHITEFISH CAVIAR

Allow 56 g (2 oz.) per serving. Serve in a glass or crystal bowl set in another bowl filled with crushed ice. Surround with smaller bowls filled with the following:

chopped hard-cooked egg whites
chopped hard-cooked egg yolks
chopped raw onion

sour cream
lemon wedges

Serve with toast or dark rye bread (buttered), crackers, melba toast or blinis (a small Russian pancake made with yeast).

Options: caviar made from any other fish roe

⋙SOUPS AND CHOWDERS⋘

BOUILLABAISSE

1 kg	fish and shellfish (use a variety from the following selection: cod, halibut, haddock, cusk, sole, eel, rockfish, whitefish, shrimp, crab, clams, mussels, small lobster)	2 lbs.
50 mL	olive oil	¼ cup
250 mL	onion, sliced	1 cup
1 clove	garlic, minced	1 clove
2	tomatoes	2
4 to 5 sprigs	parsley	4 to 5 sprigs
5 mL	salt	1 tsp.
pinch	thyme	pinch
pinch	fennel	pinch
pinch	saffron	pinch
1	bay leaf	1
	fish stock (see index) OR	
	wine and water in equal proportions	
8 slices	French bread	8 slices

Skin and debone fish, cut into chunks. Leave clams and mussels in their shells; scrub clean. Remove the shells from shrimp, lobster and crab (except for claws); cut into bite-size pieces or leave whole if small. Peel and seed tomatoes, then cut in wedges.

In the bottom of a 4-L (4-qt.) Dutch oven or ovenproof casserole, heat the olive oil and sauté onion, garlic, tomatoes, parsley and seasonings for 5 minutes. Cover, bring to a boil and cook for 10 minutes. Remove from heat.

Layer the fish and shellfish over the vegetable mixture, then add just enough fish stock to cover. Cover the pot and bring to a boil; simmer for 10 minutes. Remove from heat.

Fish and broth may be served separately or together. To serve separately, arrange fish and shellfish attractively on a heated serving platter. Place a thick slice of French bread in each soup bowl. Strain the broth and pour over the bread. Serves 8.

CHEESY FISH SOUP

500 g	fish fillets	1 lb.
30 mL	butter	2 Tbsp.
50 mL	onion, minced	¼ cup
250 mL	green pepper, minced	1 cup
125 mL	celery, minced	½ cup
50 mL	flour	¼ cup
2 mL	salt	½ tsp.
1 mL	marjoram	¼ tsp.
dash	paprika	dash
500 mL	chicken bouillon OR stock	2 cups
250 to 500 mL	milk (depending on thickness preferred)	1 to 2 cups
125 mL	cheddar cheese, grated	½ cup
	hot buttered toast	

Cut fish into 2.5 cm (1″) cubes. In a 3-L (3-qt.) pot, melt butter and sauté onion, green pepper and celery until tender-crisp. Blend in flour, salt, marjoram and paprika. Gradually add bouillon and milk. Cook, stirring constantly, until thickened. Add fish and cheese and simmer, stirring gently, for 5 to 7 minutes. Serve immediately with hot buttered toast. Makes enough for 4 to 6 people.

Options: sole, cod, cusk, haddock or pollock (Boston bluefish)

DOGFISH-CELERY CHOWDER

500 g	dogfish fillets	1 lb.
4 slices	bacon, diced	4 slices
125 mL	onion, chopped	½ cup
250 mL	potato, cubed	1 cup
500 mL	celery, large dice	2 cups
500 mL	water	2 cups
375 to 500 mL	milk	1½ to 2 cups
5 mL	salt	1 tsp.
1 mL	pepper	¼ tsp.
1 mL	nutmeg	¼ tsp.
	hot buttered toast	

Before using dogfish, the fillets must be premarinated (see index). Then cut into cubes.

In a 3-L (3-qt.) pot, sauté bacon and onion until brown. Add potato, celery and water. Bring to a boil and simmer for 10 minutes. Add milk and seasonings and return to boil. Add dogfish cubes and simmer for 10 to 15 minutes. Test seasoning and correct if necessary. Serve immediately with hot buttered toast. Makes enough for 4 to 6 people.

Options: clams, cod, haddock, turbot or sablefish (Alaska black cod)

FILLET GUMBO

500 g	fish fillets	1 lb.
75 mL	butter	⅓ cup
500 mL	onion, chopped	2 cups
250 mL	carrot, sliced	1 cup
250 mL	green pepper, chopped	1 cup
796-mL can	tomatoes	28-oz. can
125 to 250 mL	water	½ to 1 cup
5 mL	salt	1 tsp.
1 mL	pepper	¼ tsp.
2 mL	sweet basil	½ tsp.
1	bay leaf	1
375 mL	hot cooked rice	1½ cups

In a 4-L (4-qt.) pot, melt butter and stir fry onion, carrot and green pepper for about 10 minutes until tender-crisp. Add tomatoes, water and seasonings; cook over low heat for 15 minutes.

Cut fish into 2.5 cm (1″) cubes. Add fish and rice to vegetable mixture. Cover and cook for a further 7 to 10 minutes, depending on thickness of fillets. Serves 6 to 8.

Options: red snapper or other rockfish, turbot, lingcod, cusk or pollock (Boston bluefish)

FISH STOCK

A fish head, bones and trimmings may be used to make fish stock for use in fish soups or sauces. Use those from cod, red snapper, salmon, trout or lake whitefish.

5 mL	salt	1 tsp.
1	onion, chopped	1
1 stalk	celery with leaves, chopped	1 stalk
6	white peppercorns	6
1	bay leaf	1

Wash fish bits, then put them in a large pot with cold water to cover and add salt. Bring to a boil, then skim thoroughly. Add rest of ingredients and simmer for about 45 minutes. Do not cook longer or a bitter taste will result. Strain and store until ready to use. Keeps frozen for 2 to 3 months.

MACKEREL CHOWDER

198-g can	mackerel, broken into chunks	7-oz. can
6 slices	bacon, diced	6 slices
125 mL	onion, chopped	½ cup
5 mL	salt	1 tsp.
1 mL	pepper	¼ tsp.
1 mL	thyme	¼ tsp.
375 mL	potato, diced	1½ cups
540-mL can	tomatoes	19-oz. can
500 mL to 1 L	milk (to taste)	2 to 4 cups
10 mL	butter	2 tsp.
5 mL	parsley, minced	1 tsp.

Drain fish and reserve liquid. In a 3-L (3-qt.) pot, sauté bacon until crisp. Add liquid drained from fish. Stir in onion, salt, pepper and thyme; cook until tender. Add potato; cover and cook for 10 minutes until tender. Add tomatoes, milk and fish. Bring to the boiling point but do not boil. Serve immediately with butter and minced parsley on top. Makes enough for 4 to 6 people.

Option: canned tuna

WHITEFISH CAVIAR

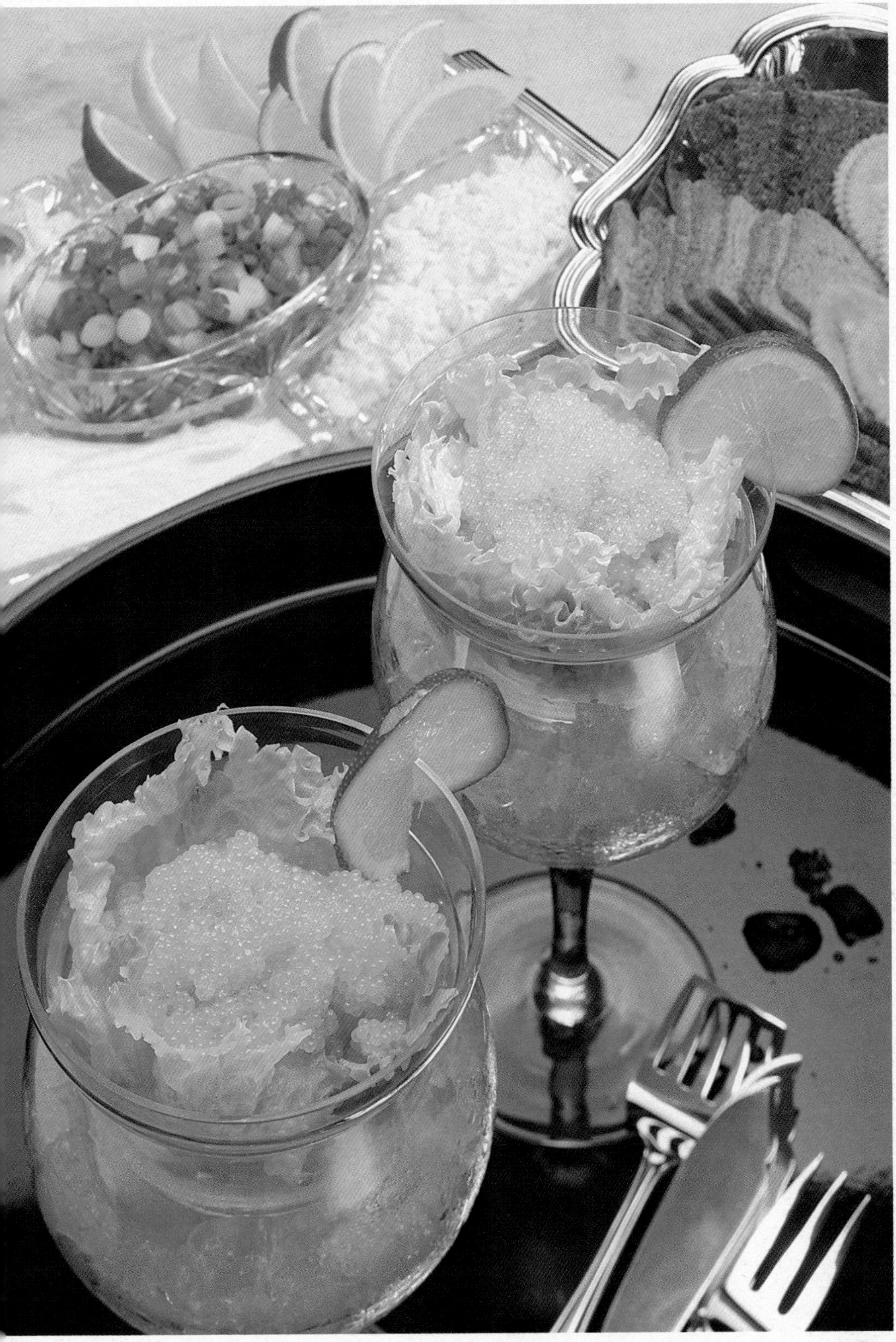

MANHATTAN CLAM CHOWDER

500 g	shelled clams with liquid OR	1 lb.
1 426-mL can	whole clams	1 15-oz. can
540-mL can	tomato juice	19-oz. can
796-mL can	tomatoes	28-oz can
750 mL	potato, diced	3 cups
250 mL	celery, chopped	1 cup
250 mL	onion, chopped	1 cup
4 slices	bacon, minced	4 slices
1	bay leaf	1
5 mL	salt	1 tsp.
1 mL	pepper	¼ tsp.
2 mL	thyme	½ tsp.
5 mL	curry powder (optional)	1 tsp.

Drain clams, reserving liquid. Chop clams.

Pour tomato juice and tomatoes into a 4-L (4-qt.) pot. Add potato, celery and onion; simmer until potato is tender.

In a pan, fry bacon lightly. Add bacon, bacon fat, chopped clams and reserved liquid to vegetable mixture. Add seasonings to taste and simmer for 5 minutes. Do not add any water. Serves 6 to 8 people.

New England Clam Chowder

36	clams in the shell OR	36
4 142-g cans	baby clams	4 5-oz. cans
4 slices	bacon, diced	4 slices
500 mL	onion, chopped	2 cups
6 medium	potatoes, diced	6 medium
5 mL	salt	1 tsp.
5 mL	celery salt	1 tsp.
4 mL	white pepper	¾ tsp.
250 mL	light cream, scalded	1 cup
500 mL	milk, scalded	2 cups
30 mL	butter	2 Tbsp.
50 mL	parsley, chopped	3 Tbsp.

Shuck fresh clams and drain, reserving liquid. Finely chop the hard parts of fresh clams and coarsely chop the soft parts. If using canned baby clams, drain and reserve liquid but leave clams whole.

In a 4-L (4-qt.) pot, fry the bacon until crisp. Remove bacon, drain and reserve. Pour off the bacon fat, leaving 75 mL (⅓ cup) in pot. Add onion and sauté over low heat for 5 minutes. Add potatoes, salt, celery salt, white pepper and reserved liquid, adding enough liquid to make 1 L (4 cups). Bring to a boil and simmer, covered, for 10 minutes. Add clams, scalded cream and milk. Bring to boiling point but do not boil. Taste and correct seasoning if necessary. Stir in butter and serve immediately topped with bacon bits and chopped parsley. Serves 12.

Oyster Stew

500 g	shucked oysters with liquid	1 pt.
50 mL	butter	3 Tbsp.
4 mL	celery salt	1 tsp.
2 mL	paprika	½ tsp.
5 mL	Worcestershire sauce	1 tsp.
250 mL	milk, scalded	1 cup
125 mL	light cream, scalded	½ cup

Melt butter in a 2-L (2-qt.) pot. Add oysters and their liquid, then blend in celery salt, paprika and Worcestershire. Bring to the boiling point. Add scalded milk and cream and bring to a boil, stirring occasionally. Pour into bowls and garnish with chopped chives or parsley. Serves 3 to 4 people.

SALT COD CHOWDER

500 g	salt cod	1 lb.
50 mL	oil	¼ cup
125 mL	onion, chopped	½ cup
125 mL	celery, diced	½ cup
75 mL	green pepper, chopped	⅓ cup
30 mL	tomato paste	2 Tbsp.
875 mL	water	3½ cups
796-mL can	tomatoes	28-oz. can
540-mL can	tomato juice	19-oz. can
175 mL	cooked rice	¾ cup
30 mL	pickling spice	2 Tbsp.
2 cloves	garlic, chopped	2 cloves
2 mL	paprika	½ tsp.
5 mL	Worcestershire sauce	1 tsp.
2 to 4 drops	Tabasco sauce	2 to 4 drops

Freshen salt cod by soaking in water overnight or for 24 hours; change water several times. (Salt cod may be soaked for 24 hours, drained, then frozen—this way, it is ready for use when needed.) Pour off water, flake cod and set aside.

In a large saucepan, heat oil and sauté onion, celery and green pepper until tender-crisp. Stir in tomato paste. Add water, tomatoes, tomato juice and rice.

Tie up pickling spice and chopped garlic in a cheesecloth bag, then add to soup. Simmer for 30 minutes. Add paprika, Worcestershire, Tabasco and flaked fish; reheat. Remove spice bag before serving. Makes enough for 12 to 15 people.

SALMON CHOWDERS

SMOKED SALMON CHOWDER

250 mL	smoked salmon, cut in chunks	1 cup
30 mL	butter	2 Tbsp.
125 mL	onion, chopped	½ cup
50 mL	celery, sliced	¼ cup
50 mL	green pepper, chopped	¼ cup
30 mL	flour	2 Tbsp.
300 mL	chicken bouillon OR stock	1¼ cups
50 mL	sour cream	¼ cup
5 mL	fresh dill, minced OR	1 tsp.
1 mL	dried dill weed	¼ tsp.
0.5 mL	pepper	⅛ tsp.
15 mL	parsley, chopped	1 Tbsp.

In a saucepan, melt butter; sauté onion, celery and green pepper. Stir in flour, then add bouillon and cook over medium heat, stirring constantly, until boiling point. Add sour cream, dill, pepper and smoked salmon; heat 2 to 3 minutes, stirring constantly. Add parsley before serving. Makes enough for 3 to 4 people.

CAMPER'S SALMON CHOWDER

250 mL	cooked salmon, flaked OR	1 cup
220-g can	salmon	7.75-oz. can
284-mL can	condensed cream of celery soup	10-oz. can
1 soup can	salmon liquid and milk OR milk	1 soup can
5 mL	curry powder	1 tsp.
	salt and pepper	

Empty contents of canned soup into saucepan. If using canned salmon, drain liquid into soup can and fill with milk. If using cooked flaked salmon, fill the soup can with milk. Add this soupcan of liquid and milk (or just milk) to the canned soup, then blend in curry powder; heat until boiling. Add salmon, broken into chunks, and season to taste. Serves 3 to 4.

SHRIMP BISQUE

1.5 kg	shrimp in the shell	3 lbs.
30 mL	butter	2 Tbsp.
125 mL	onion, chopped	½ cup
50 mL	celery, chopped	¼ cup
50 mL	carrot, chopped	¼ cup
2 sprigs	parsley	2 sprigs
1	bay leaf	1
2 sprigs	thyme	2 sprigs
2 L	fish stock (see index) OR chicken bouillon	8 cups
50 mL	dry sherry	¼ cup
50 mL	rice flour OR flour	¼ cup
5 mL	salt	1 tsp.
0.5 mL	pepper, coarsely ground	⅛ tsp.
50 mL	whipping cream	¼ cup

In a 4-L (4-qt.) pot, melt butter and sauté onion, celery, carrot, parsley, bay leaf and thyme until onion is translucent. Add shrimp in their shells and cook over high heat for 3 to 5 minutes until they turn pink and curl up. Add fish stock, bring to a boil, and simmer for 10 minutes.

Remove shrimp. Remove shells and discard. Reserve 250 mL (1 cup) shrimp for garnish. Put the rest of the shrimp, the vegetables and 250 mL (1 cup) of the stock into a blender and purée at high speed until smooth. In a bowl, soften the rice flour in 125 mL (½ cup) of the stock and set aside. Pour the remainder of the stock into a separate bowl and reserve. Rinse out the pot.

Pour purée, helped by the reserved stock, through a fine wire sieve back into the rinsed pot. Add sherry, bring to a boil, and lower heat. Pour the softened rice flour into the heated bisque, stirring constantly. Continue cooking for one more minute. Season with salt and pepper.

Just before serving, stir in whipping cream. Garnish with reserved shrimp, finely diced. Serves 10.

Options: lobster or crab

Spanish Fillet Soup

500 g	fish fillets	1 lb.
30 mL	lemon juice	2 Tbsp.
15 mL	oil	1 Tbsp.
250 mL	onion, thinly sliced	1 cup
125 mL	carrot, chopped	½ cup
125 mL	celery, chopped	½ cup
540-mL can	tomatoes	19-oz. can
250 mL	pasta spirals OR pinwheels	1 cup
625 to 750 mL	boiling water	2½ to 3 cups
5 mL	salt	1 tsp.
1 mL	pepper	¼ tsp.
1 mL	tarragon	¼ tsp.
30 mL	Parmesan cheese, grated	2 Tbsp.

Cut up fish into serving-size portions and sprinkle with lemon juice.

Heat oil in an electric frying pan or 3-L (3-qt.) saucepan; stir fry onion, carrot and celery for about 5 minutes until tender-crisp. Add tomatoes, pasta, boiling water, salt, pepper and tarragon. Simmer for 20 minutes. Place fish fillets on top and simmer 7 to 10 minutes longer. Serves 4 to 6.

To serve, place a portion of fish in each soup bowl; fill bowls with soup and sprinkle with grated Parmesan cheese.

Options: cod, sole, ocean perch, pollock (Boston bluefish) or turbot

↰SALADS↱

ALMOND-FILLET SALAD

500 g	turbot fillets	1 lb.
250 mL	celery, sliced	1 cup
250 mL	seedless green grapes (reserve some for garnish)	1 cup
50 mL	toasted almonds, slivered (reserve some for garnish)	¼ cup
50 mL	mayonnaise	¼ cup
50 mL	sour cream	¼ cup
15 mL	lemon juice	1 Tbsp.
2 mL	salt	½ tsp.
0.5 mL	white pepper	⅛ tsp.
1 mL	sweet basil	¼ tsp.
	lettuce	

Steam fish fillets, drain, and break into chunks. Add celery, grapes and almonds to fish and toss gently to mix.

In another bowl, combine mayonnaise, sour cream, lemon juice and seasonings. Fold into fish mixture. Chill for one hour before serving. Place in lettuce cups and garnish with reserved almonds and grapes. Serves 4.

Options: pollock (Boston bluefish), pickerel, sole, red snapper or haddock

AVOCADO WITH MUSSELS

125 mL	mussels, cooked OR canned	½ cup
50 mL	pickled artichoke hearts	¼ cup
2	green onions, minced	2
30 mL	mayonnaise	2 Tbsp.
10 mL	lemon juice	2 tsp.
2 medium	avocados	2 medium
	lettuce	
4 wedges	lemon	4 wedges
	parsley	

If mussels are large, cut up; if small, leave whole. Chop artichoke hearts coarsely. Blend together artichoke hearts, mussels, green onions, mayonnaise and lemon juice. Chill mixture for about one hour.

Halve avocados and remove pits. Fill each half with the mussel mixture and place on a bed of lettuce. Garnish with lemon wedges and parsley. Serves 4.

Options: cooked shrimp, crab meat or lobster

FILLET AND VEGETABLE SALAD

500 g	fish fillets	1 lb.
250 mL	cucumber, thinly sliced	1 cup
250 mL	tomato, peeled and sliced	1 cup
250 mL	onion, thinly sliced	1 cup
15 mL	vinegar	1 Tbsp.
15 mL	horseradish	1 Tbsp.
15 mL	sugar	1 Tbsp.
5 mL	salt	1 tsp.
125 mL	sour cream	½ cup

Steam the fillets, then drain and cool. Break into chunks and set aside.

In one bowl, mix together cucumber, tomato and onion. In another bowl, combine vinegar, horseradish, sugar and salt with sour cream. Pour this dressing over the vegetable mixture, tossing to mix thoroughly. Add fish last and toss gently. Chill for one hour before serving. Makes enough for 4.

Options: red snapper and other rockfish, cod, sole, turbot or pollock (Boston bluefish)

GOURMET HALIBUT MOUSSE

500 g	halibut	1 lb.
500 mL	boiling water	2 cups
2 slices	onion	2 slices
4 slices	lemon	4 slices
5 mL	salt	1 tsp.
3 whole	peppercorns	3 whole
50 mL	lemon juice	¼ cup
1 pkg.	unflavoured gelatin	1 pkg.
50 mL	vinegar	¼ cup
2 mL	salt	½ tsp.
250 mL	cucumber, peeled, seeded, diced	1 cup
50 mL	green pepper, chopped	¼ cup
50 mL	stuffed olives, sliced	¼ cup
	(reserve some for garnish)	
5 mL	fresh dill, minced OR	1 tsp.
2 mL	dried dill weed	½ tsp.
250 mL	mayonnaise	1 cup
	lettuce	
	parsley sprigs	

Poach halibut in boiling water with onion, lemon, 5 mL (1 tsp.) salt and peppercorns for 10 minutes for each 2.5 cm (1″) of thickness of fillets. Drain and cool, reserving stock. Flake the halibut.

Pour lemon juice into a saucepan and sprinkle with gelatin, stirring over low heat for about 3 minutes until dissolved.

Strain and measure reserved stock, adding water if necessary to make 500 mL (2 cups). Heat to boiling. Add gelatin, vinegar and 2 mL (½ tsp.) salt, stirring constantly. Remove from heat and chill until slightly thickened.

Fold into gelatin mixture the flaked fish, cucumber, green pepper, olives, dill and mayonnaise. Pour into individual molds and chill until firm. Unmold onto lettuce and garnish with reserved sliced stuffed olives and parsley sprigs. Serves 6 to 8.

Options: most other white-fleshed fish fillets such as cod, rockfish, turbot, cusk, carp, pickerel or wolffish

HAWAIIAN CRAB SALAD

250 g	cooked crab meat	½ lb.
1 medium	fresh papaya, cut in chunks OR	1 medium
398-mL can	papaya chunks, drained	14-oz. can
125 mL	celery, diced	½ cup
75 mL	toasted almonds, halved	⅓ cup
50 mL	green pepper, diced	¼ cup
175 mL	fresh pineapple, cut in chunks OR	¾ cup
	canned pineapple chunks, drained	
50 mL	toasted coconut, shredded	¼ cup
125 mL	mayonnaise	½ cup
15 mL	lemon juice	1 Tbsp.
4 mL	curry powder	¾ tsp.
2 mL	salt	½ tsp.
0.5 mL	white pepper	⅛ tsp.
	lettuce, shredded	
	toasted coconut, shredded	

If using fresh pineapple, you may wish to cut it in half and remove the fruit to leave 2 empty half shells in which to serve this salad.

Drain crab meat and break into chunks. Add papaya, celery, almonds, green pepper, pineapple and coconut. Refrigerate.

In another bowl, combine mayonnaise, lemon juice, curry powder, salt and pepper; mix well. Refrigerate.

When ready to serve, toss together the crab meat and mayonnaise mixtures. Place on a bed of shredded lettuce and garnish with shredded coconut. Serves 4 to 6.

Options: lobster or shrimp

MACKEREL-TOMATO STARS

425-g can	mackerel	15-oz. can
15 mL	lemon juice	1 Tbsp.
375 mL	cabbage, shredded	1½ cups
50 mL	green pepper, chopped	¼ cup
15 mL	green onion, chopped	1 Tbsp.
5 mL	salt	1 tsp.
2 mL	chili powder	½ tsp.
50 mL	mayonnaise OR salad dressing	¼ cup
4	tomatoes	4
	lettuce	
2	hard-cooked eggs, sliced	2
	green onion, chopped	

Drain and break the mackerel into bite-size pieces. Sprinkle fish with lemon juice. Toss fish with cabbage, green pepper and green onion; refrigerate.

In another bowl, mix together salt, chili powder and mayonnaise; refrigerate.

When ready to serve, blend fish and mayonnaise mixtures. Cut each tomato into 8 wedges, leaving core intact; spread apart wedges to form a star. Place each tomato star on a bed of lettuce on a plate and fill with the mackerel salad mixture. Garnish with slices of hard-cooked egg and chopped green onion. Serves 4.

Options: canned tuna or salmon

ROCKFISH SALAD DELUXE

500 g	rockfish fillets	1 lb.
125 mL	mayonnaise	½ cup
30 mL	lemon juice	2 Tbsp.
5 mL	salt	1 tsp.
0.5 mL	white pepper	⅛ tsp.
2 mL	sweet basil	½ tsp.
125 mL	orange, peeled, thinly sliced	½ cup
50 mL	celery, diced	¼ cup
15 mL	green onion, minced	1 Tbsp.
1	avocado, peeled and diced	1
50 mL	cucumber, pared and diced	¼ cup
2	hard-cooked eggs, cut in wedges	2
	lettuce	
	lemon wedges	

Steam rockfish fillets. Cool, drain and flake. Blend mayonnaise with lemon juice, salt, white pepper and basil. Add orange, celery, green onion, avocado and cucumber. Gently toss the flaked fish into this mixture. Chill for about one hour before serving. Place on a bed of lettuce garnished with wedges of hard-cooked egg and lemon. Serves 4.

Options: other firm white-fleshed fish fillets such as halibut, lake whitefish, pickerel, cod or cusk

SALMON WALDORF SALAD

250 mL	cooked salmon OR	1 cup
220-g can	sockeye OR coho salmon	7.75-oz. can
50 mL	mayonnaise	¼ cup
50 mL	sour cream	¼ cup
15 mL	vinegar	1 Tbsp.
2 mL	salt	½ tsp.
1 mL	tarragon	¼ tsp.
250 mL	apple, unpeeled, diced	1 cup
250 mL	celery, sliced	1 cup
125 mL	raisins	½ cup
50 mL	walnuts, chopped	¼ cup
	lettuce	

Drain salmon and break into bite-size pieces. In another bowl, blend mayonnaise with sour cream, vinegar, salt and tarragon. Gently toss dressing with salmon, apple, celery, raisins and walnuts. Place salad in lettuce cups. Serves 4 to 5.

Options: canned tuna or mackerel

SCALLOP CEVICHE

500 g	raw scallops	1 lb.
	fresh lemon OR lime juice	
2	tomatoes, peeled, seeded, chopped	2
4 to 6	green onions, minced	4 to 6
1	avocado, peeled and diced	1
2 mL	salt	½ tsp.
0.5 mL	pepper	⅛ tsp.
dash	Tabasco sauce	dash
	lettuce	

Coarsely chop the raw scallops and cover with fresh lemon or lime juice. Cover and let marinate in the refrigerator for several hours, until the scallops lose their translucent appearance. Drain.

Mix together the tomatoes, green onions, avocado, salt, pepper and Tabasco. Add scallops and chill for 1 to 2 hours. Place on a bed of lettuce. As a salad, serves 2 to 3; as an appetizer, serves 6.

SCANDINAVIAN HERRING SALAD

2 whole OR	pickled herring,	2 whole OR
4 fillets	drained and diced	4 fillets
2 medium	potatoes, parboiled and diced	2 medium
250 mL	celery, chopped	1 cup
50 mL	dill cucumber, diced	¼ cup
250 mL	apple, unpeeled, diced	1 cup
15 mL	onion, minced	1 Tbsp.
250 mL	cooked OR canned beets, diced	1 cup
175 mL	sour cream	¾ cup
15 mL	honey	1 Tbsp.
30 mL	lemon juice	2 Tbsp.
2	hard-cooked eggs, cut in wedges	2
30 mL	parsley, minced	2 Tbsp.
30 mL	cooked OR canned beets, minced	2 Tbsp.

Gently toss together herring, potatoes, celery, dill cucumber, apple, onion and beets. In another bowl, whip sour cream with honey and lemon juice. Combine herring and sour cream mixtures, then let stand one hour in a cool place.

Place herring salad in a flat serving bowl and decorate with wedges of hard-cooked eggs, minced parsley and minced beets. Serves 6.

SHRIMP SALAD IN ASPIC

250 mL	shelled cooked OR canned shrimp	1 cup
50 mL	lime juice	¼ cup
1 pkg.	unflavoured gelatin	1 pkg.
250 mL	water	1 cup
10 mL	honey	2 tsp.
113-g pkg.	cream cheese, softened	4-oz. pkg.
125 mL	mayonnaise	1 cup
15 mL	vinegar	1 Tbsp.
500 mL	celery, diced	2 cups
30 mL	green onion, chopped	2 Tbsp.
15 mL	fresh mint, minced	1 Tbsp.
2 mL	salt	½ tsp.
125 mL	whipping cream	½ cup
	lettuce	

If using canned shrimp, drain, rinse under cold running water, and drain again. Set shrimp aside.

Pour lime juice into a saucepan and sprinkle gelatin over it, stirring over low heat until dissolved. Remove from heat.

Boil the water in another saucepan, add honey and gelatin, stirring constantly over low heat until blended. Remove from heat and let stand until it begins to set.

Beat softened cream cheese with mayonnaise and vinegar. Add gelatin and beat until well blended. Add celery, green onion, shrimp, mint and salt; stir until well mixed.

In a bowl, beat whipping cream until stiff and fold into the salad. Pour into a mold and refrigerate until set. Unmold onto a bed of lettuce. Serves 4 to 6.

Options: cooked or canned salmon, broken into chunks

SKATE SALAD

1 kg	skate wings	2 lbs.
500 g	cottage cheese, creamed style	2 cups
125 mL	cooked snow peas, sliced	½ cup
125 mL	red pepper, julienned	½ cup
50 mL	green onion, thinly sliced	¼ cup
50 mL	almonds, sliced	¼ cup
15 mL	lemon juice	1 Tbsp.
2 mL	salt	½ tsp.
0.5 mL	pepper	⅛ tsp.
1 mL	dried dill weed	¼ tsp.
	lettuce	
	tomato wedges	
	parsley	

Poach the skate wings in a court bouillon (see index). Drain and scrape the flesh off the cartilage bones; cut flesh into bite-size pieces.

Combine cottage cheese, snow peas, red pepper, green onion, almonds and lemon juice. Season to taste with salt, pepper and dill. Carefully fold in the skate. Heap salad onto lettuce cups and decorate with tomato wedges and parsley. Serves 4.

SMOKED SALMON SALAD

500 g	barbecue-smoked salmon	1 lb.
125 mL	sour cream	½ cup
75 mL	cucumber, peeled, seeded and diced	⅓ cup
50 mL	almonds, slivered	¼ cup
30 mL	chives, chopped	2 Tbsp.
2 mL	salt	½ tsp.
0.5 mL	white pepper	⅛ tsp.
2 mL	dried dill weed	½ tsp.
	lettuce	

Cut up salmon into bite-size pieces. Toss gently with sour cream, cucumber, almonds, chives, salt, pepper and dill. Heap onto lettuce cups. Serves 3 to 4.

Options: cooked salmon or halibut

SQUID AND ZUCCHINI SALAD

500 g	squid tubes	1 lb.
125 mL	plain yogurt	½ cup
50 mL	mayonnaise OR salad dressing	¼ cup
250 mL	zucchini, diced	1 cup
125 mL	celery, diced	½ cup
50 mL	carrot, grated	¼ cup
15 mL	lemon juice	1 Tbsp.
5 mL	Worcestershire sauce	1 tsp.
dash	Tabasco sauce	dash
2 mL	salt	½ tsp.
1 mL	paprika	¼ tsp.
	lettuce	

See index for squid preparation techniques. Simmer cleaned squid tubes in boiling, salted water for one hour (or pressure cook for 5 minutes). Drain and cut into rings. Mix all other ingredients together until well blended. Stir in squid and chill for at least one hour. Spoon into lettuce cups. Serves 4 to 6.

TUNA POTATO SALAD

2 198-g cans	albacore tuna, solid	2 7-oz. cans
1 L	cooked potato, diced	4 cups
1 small	onion, chopped	1 small
30 mL	parsley, minced	2 Tbsp.
250 mL	celery, diced	1 cup
5 mL	salt	1 tsp.
30 mL	light cream	2 Tbsp.
50 mL	sour cream	¼ cup
50 mL	prepared mustard	¼ cup
10 mL	honey	2 tsp.
30 mL	lemon juice	2 Tbsp.
1 mL	thyme	¼ tsp.
0.5 mL	white pepper	⅛ tsp.

Drain tuna and break into bite-size chunks. Toss fish lightly with potato, onion, parsley, celery and salt.

In another bowl, combine light cream with sour cream, mustard, honey, lemon juice, thyme and pepper. Beat until light and fluffy. Pour over fish mixture and toss gently until well mixed. Cover and let stand about one hour in the refrigerator. Serves 6 to 8.

Option: canned salmon

෨LIGHT ENTREES෨

ABALONE STEAKS, PAN-FRIED

Abalone steaks may be served as either a light entrée or an hors d'oeuvre. To serve 4 as a light entrée, cook 500 kg (1 lb.) of abalone steaks. The same amount will serve 12 to 16 as an hors d'oeuvre.

First dip the abalone steaks into lightly beaten egg, then into breadcrumbs seasoned with your favourite herbs—or use any of the breadings in this book (see index).

Preheat 2.5 mm (⅛″) of vegetable oil in a frying pan and cook for not more than one minute on each side or until golden brown. Serve with a complementary sauce such as tartare (see index). When prepared as an hors d'oeuvre, seafood cocktail sauce (see index) makes a good dip.

ABALONE STEW

250 g	shucked abalone, cut in chunks	½ lb.
50 mL	oil	¼ cup
250 mL	onion, chopped	1 cup
125 mL	mushrooms, sliced	½ cup
50 mL	green pepper, chopped	¼ cup
213-mL can	tomato sauce	7-oz. can
175 mL	water	¾ cup
375 mL	potato, diced	1½ cups
125 mL	celery, chopped	½ cup
2 mL	salt	½ tsp.
0.5 mL	pepper	⅛ tsp.
1 mL	dried dill weed	¼ tsp.

In a large saucepan, heat oil and sauté onion until translucent. Add mushrooms and green pepper, then cook for a further 2 minutes. Add tomato sauce, water, potato and celery. Season with salt, pepper and dill. Simmer for about 7 minutes until potato is almost done. Add more water if necessary. Stir in abalone and cook over low heat for 5 to 10 minutes more or until the abalone is tender. Serves 4.

BAKED FILLET CUSTARD

500 g	cooked fish fillets, flaked	1 lb.
30 mL	green pepper, minced	2 Tbsp.
15 mL	green onion, minced	1 Tbsp.
4	eggs, well beaten	4
500 mL	light cream	2 cups
5 mL	salt	1 tsp.
1 mL	white pepper	¼ tsp.
0.5 mL	nutmeg	⅛ tsp.
0.5 mL	lemon rind, grated	⅛ tsp.

Combine flaked fish, green pepper and green onion. Place in a well-greased casserole dish. In a bowl, beat eggs well, then add cream, salt, pepper, nutmeg and lemon rind. Pour this egg mixture over the fish.

Preheat oven to 180°C (350°F) and bake fish for 30 to 35 minutes or until set in the centre. Serves 4.

Options: most white-fleshed fish fillets such as cod, rockfish, sole or turbot

CLAM SOUFFLE

125 g	shelled clams with liquid OR	4 oz.
128-g can	minced clams	5 oz. can
3 slices	bacon, diced	3 slices
50 mL	butter	¼ cup
50 mL	flour	¼ cup
250 mL	milk	1 cup
3	eggs, separated	3
2 mL	Worcestershire sauce	½ tsp.
5 mL	salt	1 tsp.
1 mL	white pepper	¼ tsp.
1 mL	rosemary	¼ tsp.

Drain clams, reserving liquid. If necessary, add water to liquid to make 125 mL (½ cup). If using fresh clams, mince.

Sauté diced bacon, drain and set aside. In a saucepan, melt butter, add flour and blend well. Gradually add milk, stirring constantly over medium heat until the sauce thickens. Add clams, reserved liquid and bacon. Continue to cook over medium heat, stirring, for 5 minutes. Remove from heat, add Worcestershire, salt, pepper and rosemary; cool slightly.

Beat egg yolks well, add to clam mixture and cook for 5 minutes over medium heat, stirring constantly. Remove from heat and cool for 5 minutes.

Beat egg whites until stiff but not dry and fold into the clam mixture. Pour into a greased baking dish placed in a pan of hot water.

Preheat oven to 190°C (375°F) and bake soufflé for 45 to 50 minutes or until it tests done in the centre. Serves 3.

Options: fresh or canned oysters

DOGFISH AND MUSHROOM CASSEROLE

500 g	dogfish fillets	1 lb.
30 mL	butter	2 Tbsp.
125 mL	mushrooms, sliced	½ cup
30 mL	flour	2 Tbsp.
250 mL	milk	1 cup
15 mL	lemon juice	1 Tbsp.
10 mL	prepared mustard	2 tsp.
5 mL	Worcestershire sauce	1 tsp.
2 mL	salt	½ tsp.
1 mL	pepper	¼ tsp.
125 mL	dry breadcrumbs	½ cup
30 mL	Parmesan cheese, grated	2 Tbsp.
15 mL	melted butter	1 Tbsp.

Before using dogfish, the fillets must be premarinated (see index). Then cut into cubes.

Melt butter in a saucepan and sauté mushrooms for 2 minutes. Stir in flour and gradually add milk, stirring over medium heat until thickened and cooked.

In a bowl, mix together lemon juice, mustard, Worcestershire, salt and pepper, then blend into the mushroom sauce. Heat to boiling and add fish. Stir gently and continue heating for 5 minutes. Pour into a lightly greased casserole dish.

In a bowl, combine breadcrumbs, grated Parmesan cheese and melted butter. Sprinkle evenly over fish mixture in the casserole dish.

Preheat oven to 180°C (350°F) and bake casserole for 15 minutes or until bubbly. Serves 4.

Options: other white-fleshed fish fillets

EEL CASSEROLE

1 kg	eels	2 lbs.
1 L	iced water	1 qt.
30 mL	salt	2 Tbsp.
30 mL	oil	2 Tbsp.
125 mL	onion, chopped	½ cup
500 mL	potato, diced	2 cups
250 mL	carrot, diced	1 cup
125 mL	celery, diced	½ cup
50 mL	uncooked rice	¼ cup
	salt and pepper	
30 mL	butter	2 Tbsp.
30 mL	flour	2 Tbsp.
250 mL	reserved liquid	1 cup
125 mL	cheddar cheese, grated	½ cup

If not already dressed, remove head and entrails from eels. Soak eels for 10 minutes in iced water to which salt has been added, then pull off skin. Split the eels open by cutting along the top of the backbone. Next, cut under the backbone and remove. Cut eels into pieces 4 cm (1½″) long.

Heat oil in a large saucepan and sauté onion until tender. Add eels, potato, carrot, celery, rice, and salt and pepper to taste. Add boiling water to cover, if necessary, and simmer until vegetables are cooked. Drain, reserving 250 mL (1 cup) of the liquid.

Melt butter in a saucepan, add flour, then stir in reserved liquid, cooking over medium heat until thickened. Stir this sauce into the eel and vegetable mixture and pour into a lightly greased casserole dish. Top with grated cheese.

Preheat oven to 180°C (350°F) and bake casserole for 15 to 20 minutes or until nicely browned. Serves 4.

FILLET AND CARROT SOUFFLE

250 g	cooked fish fillets, flaked	1 cup
50 mL	butter	¼ cup
50 mL	flour	¼ cup
5 mL	salt	1 tsp
0.5 mL	pepper	⅛ tsp.
250 mL	milk	1 cup
125 mL	sour cream	½ cup
15 mL	lemon juice	1 Tbsp.
50 mL	carrot, grated	¼ cup
15 mL	parsley, minced	1 Tbsp.
3	eggs, separated	3

In a saucepan, melt butter, then stir in flour, salt and pepper. Gradually add milk and cook over medium heat, stirring until it thickens. Remove from heat and add sour cream, lemon juice, carrot and parsley.

Beat egg yolks in a bowl and add them to the sauce. Heat sauce, stirring constantly until thickened. Remove from heat and cool for 5 minutes. Add flaked fish.

Beat egg whites in a bowl until stiff but not dry, then fold into fish mixture. Pour into a greased 1.5-L (1½-qt.) casserole. Place dish in a shallow pan of hot water.

Preheat oven to 180°C (350°F) and bake soufflé for about 45 minutes or until set. Serves 4.

Options: white-fleshed fish such as cod, sole, red snapper, turbot or cusk

FILLET AND CHEESE SOUFFLE

500 g	fillets	1 lb.
30 mL	butter	2 Tbsp.
30 mL	flour	2 Tbsp.
250 mL	light cream	1 cup
125 mL	cheddar cheese, grated	½ cup
3	eggs, separated	3
5 mL	salt	1 tsp.
0.5 mL	pepper	⅛ tsp.
0.5 mL	nutmeg	⅛ tsp.

Steam fillets, drain, cool and flake. To make sauce, melt butter in a saucepan and add flour. Gradually pour in light cream, stirring constantly over medium heat until thickened. Add cheese and stir till melted.

In a bowl, lightly beat egg yolks and add a little of the hot sauce. Then stir the yolk mixture into the rest of the sauce. Add salt, pepper and nutmeg to taste, then stir in flaked fish. Remove this mixture from heat and cool slightly.

In a bowl, beat egg whites until stiff but not dry, then fold into fish and sauce mixture. Pour into a greased soufflé dish or straight-sided casserole, placed in a shallow pan of hot water.

Preheat oven to 190°C (375°F) and bake soufflé for 45 minutes to 1 hour until it tests done in the centre. Serve immediately. Makes enough for 4.

Options: most white-fleshed fish such as red snapper, cod, pollock (Boston bluefish), turbot or lake whitefish

Fillet and Mushroom Rarebit

500 g	fish fillets, cubed	1 lb.
50 mL	butter	¼ cup
500 mL	mushrooms, sliced	2 cups
30 mL	flour	2 Tbsp.
250 mL	light cream	1 cup
500 mL	mild cheese, grated	2 cups
5 mL	Worcestershire sauce	1 tsp.
3 drops	Tabasco sauce	3 drops
2 mL	salt	½ tsp.
0.5 mL	white pepper	⅛ tsp.
1	egg	1
	hot biscuits OR toast points	

Melt butter in a saucepan and sauté mushrooms for 2 to 3 minutes until tender. Push mushrooms to one side and blend in flour. Gradually pour in cream, stirring over low heat until thick and smooth. Add cheese, stirring until melted. Season with Worcestershire, Tabasco, salt and pepper. Remove from heat.

Beat egg in a small bowl and blend in small amount of cheese sauce. Pour this egg mixture into the cheese sauce, then add fish. Simmer gently and stir continuously for 5 minutes or until fish is cooked. Serve on hot biscuits or toast points. Makes enough for 4 to 6.

Options: halibut, turbot, cusk, lake whitefish or carp

FILLET AND TOMATO CASSEROLE

500 g	fish fillets	1 lb.
15 mL	butter	1 Tbsp.
125 mL	onion, thinly sliced	½ cup
125 mL	green pepper, thinly sliced	½ cup
540-mL can	stewed tomatoes	19-oz. can
30 mL	parsley, chopped	2 Tbsp.
2 mL	salt	½ tsp.
1 mL	pepper	¼ tsp.
30 mL	melted butter	2 Tbsp.

Melt 15 mL (1 Tbsp.) butter in a frying pan and sauté onion and green pepper for 5 minutes.

Pour tomatoes in a flat baking dish, then layer with onion and green pepper. Place fish fillets on top of the vegetables. Sprinkle with parsley, salt and pepper. Drizzle with melted butter and cover.

Preheat oven to 230°C (450°F) and bake according to the timing rule (see index). Serves 4 to 5.

Options: cod, sole, rockfish, halibut, pickerel or turbot

FILLETS WITH CREAMY CUCUMBER TOPPING

500 g	fish fillets	1 lb.
50 mL	prepared creamy cucumber dressing OR any creamy salad dressing	¼ cup
30 mL	parsley, minced	2 Tbsp.
1 mL	salt	¼ tsp.
0.5 mL	white pepper	⅛ tsp.

Place fillets in a single layer in a greased, shallow baking dish. In a bowl, blend creamy cucumber dressing with parsley, salt and pepper. Spread over fillets.

Preheat oven to 230°C (450°F) and bake fillets according to the timing rule (see index). Serves 3.

Golden Pan-Fried Rainbow Trout

6 pan-size	rainbow trout, dressed	6 pan-size
12 slices	bacon	12 slices
1	egg	1
50 mL	milk	¼ cup
5 mL	salt	1 tsp.
0.5 mL	pepper	⅛ tsp.
125 mL	flour	½ cup
50 mL	yellow cornmeal	¼ cup
5 mL	paprika	1 tsp.

Rinse trout under cold running water and pat dry. Fry bacon until crisp and remove from pan, reserving the bacon fat. Keep the bacon warm in the oven.

In a bowl, beat the egg lightly, then add milk, salt and pepper.

In another bowl, combine the flour, cornmeal and paprika.

Dip the fish first in the egg mixture, then coat in the flour mixture. Fry in hot reserved bacon fat (add more fat if necessary) for 2 to 3 minutes on each side or until the fish are golden brown and test done. Drain fish on paper towels and garnish with bacon. Serves 6.

Option: 500-g (1-lb.) baby coho salmon

LOBSTER THERMIDOR

4 250-g	lobster tails	4 8-oz.
2 to 3 L	water	2 to 3 qts.
1	onion, coarsely chopped	1
1	lemon, sliced	1
1 stalk	celery, coarsely chopped	1 stalk
1	bay leaf	1
30 mL	melted butter	2 Tbsp.
50 mL	butter	¼ cup
30 mL	chives, snipped	2 Tbsp.
50 mL	flour	¼ cup
150 mL	light cream	⅔ cup
50 mL	medium-dry sherry	¼ cup
2 mL	dry mustard	½ tsp.
2 mL	salt	½ tsp.
0.5 mL	pepper	⅛ tsp.
50 mL	Parmesan cheese, grated	¼ cup
	parsley sprigs	

Pour the water into a large pot. Add onion, lemon, celery and bay leaf, then bring to a boil. Reduce heat and simmer for 10 minutes. Add lobster tails and bring to boil again. Skim off any foam and simmer for 6 minutes. Remove lobster tails and set aside to cool. Strain broth and reserve 125 mL (½ cup) liquid.

While lobster tails are still warm, remove meat from shell and cut into bite-size pieces. Clean the shells and brush inside and out with the melted butter.

In a saucepan, melt butter and sauté chives for one minute. Stir in flour. Gradually add the light cream and reserved broth, stirring over medium heat until thickened and cooked. Add sherry and mustard and cook, stirring, for one more minute. Season to taste with salt and pepper. Add lobster meat to the sauce.

Place shells on a greased broiler pan and spoon the lobster mixture into them. Sprinkle with Parmesan cheese and put under the broiler until golden and bubbly. Garnish with sprigs of parsley. Serves 4.

ROCKFISH CROQUETTES

500 g	rockfish fillets	1 lb.
125 mL	mashed potato	½ cup
30 mL	butter	2 Tbsp.
75 mL	cheddar cheese, grated	⅓ cup
30 mL	onion, grated	2 Tbsp.
1	egg, beaten	1
30 mL	lemon juice	2 Tbsp.
2 mL	salt	½ tsp.
1 mL	tarragon	¼ tsp.
125 mL	cracker crumbs OR crushed cornflakes	½ cup

Steam rockfish fillets, drain, cool and flake. Mix mashed potato with butter, then combine all ingredients except crumbs.

Shape fish mixture into 6 individual patties and roll in the crumbs. These croquettes may be either baked or pan fried.

To bake, preheat oven to 180°C (350°F) and cook croquettes on a greased pan for 25 to 30 minutes. To pan fry, preheat 6 mm (¼″) oil and cook for 3 to 5 minutes each side or until golden brown. Serve with a favourite sauce, such as sherry-mushroom cream sauce (see index). Makes enough for 6.

Options: most other white-fleshed fish such as cod, sole or lake whitefish

ROE

DEEP-FRIED ROE

Roe may be deep fried using any breading or batter (see index). Preheat vegetable oil to 190°C (375°F) and deep fry for 2 to 3 minutes, depending on the size of the roe. Try serving deep-fried roe with hollandaise sauce (see index).

HERB-BAKED ROE

350 g	roe	12 oz.
250 mL	whipping cream	1 cup
1 mL	rosemary	¼ tsp.
1 mL	chervil	¼ tsp.
2 mL	salt	½ tsp.
1 thin slice	onion, separated into rings	1 thin slice
1	bay leaf	1
5 mL	parsley, chopped	1 tsp.

Place roe in a well-greased, small casserole dish. Blend whipping cream with the rosemary, chervil and salt, then pour over the roe (it should just cover). Top with onion rings, bay leaf and parsley.

Preheat oven to 180°C (350°F). Cover and bake roe for 20 to 25 minutes. After baking, discard onion rings and bay leaf. Serves 2.

SAUTEED ROE

350 g	roe	12 oz.
25 mL	flour	2 Tbsp.
1 mL	salt	¼ tsp.
1 mL	pepper	¼ tsp.
0.5 mL	rosemary	⅛ tsp.
2 slices	bacon OR	2 slices
25 mL	butter	2 Tbsp.

Combine flour, salt, pepper and rosemary. Dust roe lightly with this seasoned flour. In a frying pan, sauté the bacon until golden and crisp, then remove and keep warm.

Fry the roe in bacon fat for about 2 to 3 minutes on each side until done and serve with bacon. Or, melt butter in a frying pan and sauté the roe over medium heat until golden brown on both sides.

SALMON AND CHEESE LOAF

2 220-g cans	pink salmon	2 7.75-oz. cans
1	egg	1
250 mL	medium cheddar cheese, grated	1 cup
250 mL	soft breadcrumbs	1 cup
15 mL	onion, minced	1 Tbsp.
15 mL	butter, melted	1 Tbsp.
2 mL	salt	½ tsp.
0.5 mL	pepper	⅛ tsp.
2 mL	sweet basil	½ tsp.
50 mL	medium cheddar cheese, grated, for topping	¼ cup

Drain salmon, reserving liquid. Flake salmon and crush bones. In a bowl, beat egg. Add salmon, reserved liquid, grated cheese, breadcrumbs, onion, melted butter, salt, pepper and basil. Pour into a greased loaf pan.

Preheat oven to 180°C (350°F) and bake fish for 20 minutes. Top with grated cheese and return to oven for a further 10 to 15 minutes. Serves 4.

Options: canned tuna or mackerel

SALMON PIZZA

220-g can	pink salmon	7.75-oz. can
125 mL	milk and salmon liquid	½ cup
500 mL	biscuit mix (one that needs only milk to be added)	2 cups
213-mL can	tomato sauce	7.5-oz. can
340-g pkg.	mozzarella cheese, thinly sliced	12-oz. pkg.
250 mL	onion, minced	1 cup
125 mL	black olives, minced	½ cup
50 mL	green pepper, minced	¼ cup
1 mL	orégano	¼ tsp.
	salt and pepper	
50 mL	Parmesan cheese, grated	¼ cup

Drain salmon and reserve liquid, adding enough milk to make 125 mL (½ cup) of liquid. Blend together biscuit mix and liquid to make a dough. Knead several times and roll into a circle 30 cm (12″) in diameter to fit a pizza pan.

Spread the tomato sauce on the dough. Layer with mozzarella cheese, flaked salmon, onion, olives and green pepper. Season with orégano, salt and pepper. Top with Parmesan cheese.

Preheat oven to 230°C (450°F) and bake pizza for 15 to 20 minutes. Serves 3 to 4.

SALT COD ESPAGNOLE

500 g	salt cod	1 lb.
30 mL	olive OR salad oil	2 Tbsp.
1 small	onion, chopped	1 small
1 clove	garlic, mashed	1 clove
30 mL	parsley, minced	2 Tbsp.
540-mL can	stewed tomatoes	19-oz. can
250 mL	chicken bouillon OR stock	1 cup
500 mL	potato, diced	2 cups
1	canned pimento, chopped	1
125 mL	dry breadcrumbs	½ cup
15 mL	melted butter	1 Tbsp.
	pepper	

Freshen salt cod by soaking in cold water overnight or for 24 hours, changing the water several times.

In a saucepan, heat oil and sauté onion and garlic until tender. Add parsley and cook for one minute more. Add stewed tomatoes and bouillon, then season to taste. (Do not add any salt until you taste this mixture first.) Add potato and pimento and mix well.

Drain fish and place in a greased, shallow baking dish. Pour the sauce mixture over fish. Combine breadcrumbs with melted butter, then sprinkle over the top.

Preheat oven to 180°C (350°F) and bake uncovered for 25 to 30 minutes. Serves 4 to 6.

SCALLOPED SHRIMP

250 mL	shelled cooked OR canned shrimp	1 cup
50 mL	butter	¼ cup
50 mL	flour	¼ cup
500 mL	light cream	2 cups
2 mL	salt	½ tsp.
0.5 mL	pepper	⅛ tsp.
1 mL	ginger powder	¼ tsp.
4	hard-cooked eggs, chopped	4
5 mL	parsley, chopped	1 tsp.
125 mL	breadcrumbs	½ cup
15 mL	melted butter	1 Tbsp.
	hot buttered toast OR hot fluffy rice	

If using canned shrimp, drain, rinse under cold running water, and drain again.

In a saucepan, melt butter, add flour, and stir to blend. Gradually pour in light cream and cook over medium heat, stirring constantly, until thick and smooth. Add salt, pepper and ginger. Stir hard-cooked eggs, shrimp and parsley into sauce, then pour into a greased baking dish. Combine breadcrumbs with melted butter, then sprinkle over the casserole.

Preheat oven to 180°C (350°F) and bake for 15 minutes or until bubbly. Serve on hot buttered toast or with fluffy rice. Makes enough for 4.

Options: fresh or canned crab or lobster

SEAFOOD AND CREAM CHEESE OMELETTE

125 g	cooked salmon OR canned seafood	4 oz.
4	eggs	4
30 mL	ice-cold water	2 Tbsp.
30 mL	butter	2 Tbsp.
50 mL	cream cheese, softened	¼ cup
15 mL	dry white wine OR sherry	1 Tbsp.
2 mL	salt	½ tsp.
0.5 mL	pepper	⅛ tsp.
30 mL	green onion, minced	2 Tbsp.

Beat eggs in a bowl until light and frothy, then add the ice-cold water and beat just to mix.

Melt the butter in a frying pan and add eggs. Cook over medium heat, stirring into the centre occasionally to cook evenly.

In a bowl, beat cream cheese with wine, salt and pepper. Add green onion and seafood.

When egg is almost set, spread cheese and seafood mixture over it and let cook for another minute. Fold omelette in half and serve immediately. Makes 2 servings.

Options: cooked or canned salmon, shrimp, crab or lobster; if using canned seafood, drain and discard liquid

SEAFOOD COQUILLES

500 g	seafood	1 lb.
125 mL	water	½ cup
125 mL	dry white wine	½ cup
4 thin slices	onion	4 thin slices
4 thin slices	lemon	4 thin slices
2 sprigs	parsley	2 sprigs
1	bay leaf	1
6	peppercorns	6
5 mL	salt	1 tsp.
30 mL	butter	2 Tbsp.
50 mL	mushrooms, sliced	¼ cup
30 mL	flour	2 Tbsp.
50 mL	light cream	¼ cup
50 mL	soft breadcrumbs	¼ cup
30 mL	cheddar cheese, grated	2 Tbsp.

Bring water and wine to boil with onion, lemon, parsley, bay leaf, peppercorns and salt. Strain this court bouillon and reserve the broth if the seafood is cooked. To cook seafood in broth, bring the broth back to a boil, add seafood and simmer either in or over the liquid (in a steamer), for 5 to 7 minutes, depending on the thickness of the fish pieces. Remove the seafood, reserving the broth.

In a saucepan, melt the butter and sauté the mushrooms for 5 minutes. Blend in flour and slowly add reserved broth, stirring constantly over medium heat until thickened. Add cream and fold in seafood. If the sauce is too thick, increase the light cream until the sauce is of medium thickness. Pour into 4 to 6 greased scallop shells.

Preheat oven to 260°C (500°F) and bake for 5 to 8 minutes. Mix breadcrumbs with cheese, then sprinkle over the seafood mixture. Place under broiler for 1 to 2 minutes until golden brown. Serves 2 to 3 people as an entrée, or 4 to 6 as an appetizer.

Options: The famous Coquilles St. Jacques is made by using scallops. Try crab, shrimp or fillets of fish such as salmon, halibut, cod or turbot cut into cubes. If seafood is already cooked, simmer the court bouillon for 5 to 8 minutes without it, then drain and reserve broth.

SEAFOOD QUICHE

250 g	cooked salmon OR canned seafood	8 oz.
	pastry for pie shell	
3 slices	bacon, diced	3 slices
125 mL	cheddar cheese, grated	½ cup
30 mL	green onion, minced	2 Tbsp.
3	eggs	3
125 mL	plain yogurt	½ cup
250 mL	light cream (and salmon liquid,	1 cup
	if using canned salmon)	
2 mL	salt	½ tsp.
0.5 mL	white pepper	⅛ tsp.
0.5 mL	fennel	⅛ tsp.
	paprika	

Preheat oven to 200°C (400°F). Line a pie plate 23 cm (9″) in diameter with pastry and bake for 5 minutes. Remove from oven and allow to cool. Reduce oven temperature to 180°C (350°F).

Fry bacon until crisp, then drain on absorbent paper. Set aside.

Flake seafood and distribute evenly over bottom of pie shell. Cover the fish with bacon, cheese and green onion.

In a bowl, beat eggs and add yogurt, light cream (including salmon liquid if any), salt, pepper and fennel. Pour this mixture over the seafood and sprinkle the top with paprika. Bake at 180°C (350°F) for 45 minutes or until set in the centre. Serves 6.

Options: cooked or canned salmon, canned tuna; fresh or canned shrimp, crab or lobster (discard liquids from canned shellfish)

SKATE PORTUGAISE

1 kg	skate wings	2 lbs.
1 medium	onion, chopped	1 medium
1 clove	garlic, crushed	1 clove
1 mL	thyme	¼ tsp.
1 mL	rosemary	¼ tsp.
2 mL	salt	½ tsp.
0.5 mL	pepper	⅛ tsp.
540-mL can	stewed tomatoes	19-oz. can

Cut skate wings into serving-size pieces and place in a well-greased, shallow oven dish. Sprinkle with chopped onion. Mix together the remaining ingredients and pour over fish to cover.

Preheat oven to 180°C (350°F) and bake skate for 25 to 30 minutes or until it is done (segments part easily). Serves 4.

SMELT PARMESAN

1 kg	smelt	2 lbs.
125 mL	flour	½ cup
2 mL	salt	½ tsp.
0.5 mL	pepper	⅛ tsp.
1	egg	1
15 mL	water	1 Tbsp.
125 mL	cracker crumbs	½ cup
75 mL	Parmesan cheese, grated	⅓ cup
2 mL	salt	½ tsp.
125 mL	lemon juice	½ cup
	oil for pan frying	

Clean smelt and bone if desired. It is not necessary to bone, as the bones become crunchy after cooking.

Combine flour, 2 mL salt (½ tsp.) and pepper in a clean brown paper bag.

In a bowl, beat egg. Then add water and stir to mix.

In a second bowl, mix together cracker crumbs, Parmesan cheese and salt.

Dip each smelt in lemon juice, then shake in the bag of seasoned flour. Dip each smelt into the egg mixture, then coat in the crumb and cheese mixture. (The bag of seasoned flour may be kept and used again. The lemon juice may be kept in a separate bottle in the refrigerator and used again.)

Preheat about 6 mm (¼″) oil to 180°C (350°F) in a frying pan and cook smelt about 2 to 3 minutes each side until brown. Serves 6.

Options: capelin, silverside or eulachon

TUNA-STUFFED PEPPERS

198-g can	flaked tuna, drained	7-oz. can
6 medium	green peppers	6 medium
500 mL	cooked rice OR noodles	2 cups
75 mL	onion, chopped	⅓ cup
212-mL can	tomato sauce	7.5-oz. can
1	egg, well beaten	1
30 mL	lemon juice	2 Tbsp.
5 mL	salt	1 tsp.
0.5 mL	pepper	⅛ tsp.
0.5 mL	rosemary	⅛ tsp.
	Parmesan cheese, grated	

Cut the stem end off the green peppers and remove all seeds and membranes. Parboil peppers for 10 minutes and drain.

Prepare stuffing by combining tuna, rice, onion, tomato sauce, egg, lemon juice, salt, pepper and rosemary. Mix well to blend. Spoon this mixture into the green peppers and sprinkle tops with grated Parmesan. Place peppers in a greased baking dish.

Preheat oven to 200°C (400°F) and bake stuffed peppers for 15 minutes. Serves 6.

Options: cooked or canned salmon, mackerel, shrimp, crab or lobster; if using canned seafood, drain and discard liquid

WHITEFISH CASSEROLE

250 mL	cooked lake whitefish fillets, flaked	1 cup
250 mL	basic cream sauce (see index)	1 cup
3	egg yolks, lightly beaten	3
125 mL	crackers, crushed	½ cup
50 mL	onion, minced	¼ cup
30 mL	parsley, minced	2 Tbsp.
30 mL	lemon juice	2 Tbsp.
10 mL	horseradish	2 tsp.
10 mL	prepared mustard	2 tsp.
2 mL	salt	½ tsp.
0.5 mL	pepper	⅛ tsp.
3	egg whites, stiffly beaten	3

Combine all ingredients except egg whites. Fold in stiffly beaten egg whites. Pour mixture into a lightly greased pie plate 23 cm (9″) in diameter.

Preheat oven to 180°C (350°F) and bake casserole for 45 minutes or until set. Serves 3 to 4.

Options: most other white-fleshed fish such as cod, sole, halibut, cusk, turbot or carp

WHITEFISH FILLETS ON CLOUD NINE

1 kg	lake whitefish fillets	2 lbs.
50 mL	cream cheese, softened	¼ cup
50 mL	sour cream	¼ cup
15 mL	mayonnaise	1 Tbsp.
5 mL	lemon juice	1 tsp.
5 mL	Worcestershire sauce	1 tsp.
2 mL	dried dill weed	½ tsp.
2 mL	salt	½ tsp.
1	egg white, stiffly beaten	1

Preheat broiler. Cut fillets into serving-size portions and place on a foil-covered tray. Cook 12.5 cm (5″) below broiler for about 6 minutes, then remove.

In a bowl, beat the cream cheese and combine with all other ingredients—except the egg white—until thoroughly blended. Fold in the stiffly beaten egg white. Spread this topping over the fillets and return to the broiler to cook for a further 3 to 4 minutes or until puffed and golden. Serves 4 to 6.

Options: cod, red snapper, carp, swordfish or halibut

WINE-POACHED TROUT

4 pan-size	rainbow trout, dressed	4 pan-size
125 mL	dry white wine	½ cup
4 thin slices	onion	4 thin slices
2 thin slices	lemon	2 thin slices
1 mL	dill seeds	¼ tsp.
1 mL	rosemary	¼ tsp.
5 mL	salt	1 tsp.
2 mL	peppercorns	½ tsp.

Pour wine into frying pan, then add onion, lemon, dill, rosemary, salt and peppercorns, with enough water to cover the fish. Bring to a boil, then add trout and simmer, covered, for 10 to 15 minutes or until done. Lift fish onto heated platter and remove skin, reserving liquid. Serve hot with basic cream sauce (see index), using reserved liquid. Makes enough for 4.

MAIN COURSE
⊛ENTREES⊛

ALL-IN-ONE SALMON DINNER

1 kg	salmon fillets OR steaks	2 lbs.
6 slices	bacon, chopped	6 slices
4 medium	tomatoes, peeled and sliced	4 medium
1	onion, thinly sliced	1
375 mL	potato, thinly sliced	1½ cups
375 mL	green beans, sliced	1½ cups
10 mL	salt	2 tsp.
1 mL	pepper	¼ tsp.

Cut the fish into serving-size portions. Prepare 6 pieces of aluminum foil, each 46 cm (18″) square. In the centre of each piece of foil, arrange an equal quantity of fish, bacon, tomatoes, onion, potato and green beans. Sprinkle with salt and pepper. Wrap up each serving securely, sealing the foil well.

The fish may be cooked either on a barbecue (see index) or in the oven. Place foil packages on a bed of hot coals or preheat oven to 230°C (450°F) and bake for 15 to 20 minutes. Serves 6.

ASPIC-GLAZED WHOLE ARCTIC CHARR

Partially thaw a dressed arctic charr. Wash fish thoroughly under cold running water and pat dry with paper towels. Measure thickness of the fish in order to determine cooking time according to the timing rule (see index). Prepare enough court bouillon (see index) to cover adequately the fish in a poacher.

Wrap the fish in a piece of cheesecloth large enough to tie a loose knot at each end for use as handles. Take care that the cheesecloth is well clear of the source of heat.

Bring court bouillon to a boil in fish poacher and lower fish into the liquid. Remove any excess liquid or add more if necessary. Return liquid to a boil, then reduce and simmer according to the timing rule. When fish is cooked, lift out of the liquid by grasping the handles at each end of the cheesecloth. Carefully remove cheesecloth, then skin the fish while it is still warm. Place fish on a serving platter to cool. Refrigerate covered until thoroughly chilled before glazing. Allow 250 g (½ lb.) per person.

ASPIC GLAZE

500 mL	water	2 cups
175 mL	dry white wine	¾ cup
50 mL	white vinegar	¼ cup
1 small	onion, sliced	1 small
2 stalks	celery, tops only	2 stalks
1	lemon, juice and cut-up rind	1
1	bay leaf	1
2 mL	peppercorns	½ tsp.
5 mL	salt	1 tsp.
3 pkgs.	unflavoured gelatin	3 pkgs.
50 mL	cold water	¼ cup
2	egg whites and shells	2
	sprigs of parsley OR watercress	
	wedges of lemon OR lime	

In a large pot, mix together 500 mL (2 cups) water, wine, vinegar, onion, celery, lemon juice and rind, bay leaf, peppercorns and salt. Simmer for about 30 minutes. Remove from heat, strain, and return strained liquid to pot.

To make aspic, soften gelatin in 50 mL (¼ cup) cold water and dissolve over low heat. Add gelatin to strained liquid, stirring with a wire whisk.

Beat egg whites in a bowl until only lightly frothy. Crush egg shells (they serve to clarify the aspic). Add egg whites and crushed shells to aspic, whisking until frothy.

Over high heat, bring aspic to a vigorous boil. Remove from heat and leave to settle for 10 to 15 minutes. Strain through several layers of cheesecloth. Aspic will be crystal clear. Allow to cool until it starts to set before beginning to glaze the fish.

While the aspic is cooling, decorate the fish as desired. Some suggestions are: thinly sliced radish, cucumber, zucchini, lemon or lime, black or stuffed olives, carrot curls, chopped hard-cooked egg whites and yolks, pimento, parsley, watercress or fresh dill.

When aspic cools to the setting point, spoon it carefully over the whole fish. If aspic sets too quickly, thin by returning to heat, then allow to cool again until it starts to set. As a final touch before serving, garnish with sprigs of parsley or watercress and wedges of lemon or lime.

Options: whole dressed salmon, trout or lake whitefish

CITRUS-TOPPED FILLETS

1 kg	fish fillets	2 lbs.
30 mL	butter	2 Tbsp.
50 mL	onion, chopped	¼ cup
50 mL	celery, chopped	¼ cup
250 mL	soft breadcrumbs, toasted	1 cup
125 mL	grapefruit OR orange segments, diced	½ cup
10 mL	parsley, chopped	2 tsp.
1 mL	marjoram	¼ tsp.
2 mL	salt	½ tsp.
0.5 mL	pepper	⅛ tsp.
30 mL	grapefruit OR orange juice	2 Tbsp.

Place fillets in a single layer in a greased baking dish.

In a saucepan, melt butter, then sauté onion and celery until tender-crisp. Remove from heat and add all the remaining ingredients. Toss this mixture lightly, then spread evenly over fillets.

Preheat oven to 230°C (450°F) and bake fish for 12 to 15 minutes or until it tests done. Serves 4 to 6.

Options: most white-fleshed fish such as halibut, cod, red snapper, turbot, cusk, lake whitefish or carp

CLAM FETTUCCINE

375 g	shucked clams OR canned clams OR canned baby clams	12 oz.
750 mL	fettuccine noodles	3 cups
500 mL	whipping cream	2 cups
125 mL	light cream	½ cup
50 mL	dry white wine	¼ cup
5 mL	salt	1 tsp.
0.5 mL	pepper	⅛ tsp
1 mL	rosemary	¼ tsp.
125 mL	Parmesan cheese, grated	½ cup

Drain clams and chop. If using canned baby clams, drain but leave whole.

Following package directions, cook fettuccine in salted, boiling water to which 15 mL (1 Tbsp.) oil has been added, until "al dente," cooked but firm. Drain in a sieve and rinse under cold running water.

In a large saucepan, bring whipping cream and light cream to boil and boil rapidly for 4 to 5 minutes until reduced to ⅔. Add wine, salt, pepper and rosemary, then cook for one minute more. Add Parmesan and clams, then fettuccine, stirring over medium heat until sauce starts to boil. Remove and serve immediately. Makes enough for 4.

Options: lobster, shrimp or crab meat

COD CURRY

1 kg	cod fillets	2 lbs.
30 mL	butter	2 Tbsp.
250 mL	onion, minced	1 cup
1	bay leaf	1
1 mL	thyme	¼ tsp.
10 mL	curry powder (or to taste)	2 tsp.
30 mL	flour	2 Tbsp.
250 mL	fish stock (see index) OR milk	1 cup
50 mL	whipping cream	¼ cup
5 mL	salt	1 tsp.
1 mL	pepper	¼ tsp.
1 L	hot cooked rice	4 cups

Place fillets in a single layer in a greased baking dish.

Melt butter in a saucepan and sauté onion until translucent. Add bay leaf, thyme and curry powder; then heat, stirring, for 5 minutes. Blend in the flour, then gradually the fish stock, stirring over medium heat until thickened and cooked. Remove the bay leaf. Stir in the cream, then add salt and pepper. Pour this sauce over the fillets.

Preheat oven to 230°C (450°F) and bake fish for 15 to 20 minutes or until it tests done. Serve over hot rice. Makes 6 to 8 servings.

Options: most firm-fleshed fish such as haddock, cusk, turbot or pollock (Boston bluefish)

CURRIED SHRIMP

500 g	shelled shrimp	1 lb.
50 mL	lime OR lemon juice	¼ cup
50 mL	water	¼ cup
5 mL	salt	1 tsp.
30 mL	vegetable oil	2 Tbsp.
175 mL	onion, minced	¾ cup
250 mL	celery, minced	1 cup
15 mL	chives, chopped	1 Tbsp.
10 mL	curry powder	2 tsp.
2	tomatoes, peeled and chopped	2
50 mL	flour	¼ cup
250 mL	fish stock (see index) OR chicken bouillon	1 cup
1 L	hot cooked rice	4 cups

In a bowl, combine lime juice, water and salt. Add shrimp and marinate for 20 minutes, then drain, reserving liquid.

Heat oil in a skillet. Add onion, celery, chives and curry powder; cook for 5 minutes without browning. Add tomatoes and cook one minute more. Add flour and stir to blend. Gradually add fish stock and reserved liquid, stirring until cooked and thickened. Mix in shrimp and heat just until they are hot. Serve immediately over rice, with condiments such as sliced bananas, dried coconut flakes, tomato and onion in vinegar, raisins and pineapple chunks. Makes enough for 4.

Options: crab, lobster or scallops

DOGFISH

DEEP-FRIED DOGFISH FILLETS

750 g	dogfish fillets	1½ lbs.
175 mL	flour	¾ cup
2 mL	salt	½ tsp.
0.5 mL	pepper	⅛ tsp.
175 mL	flour	¾ cup
1	egg	1
2 mL	salt	½ tsp.
125 mL	water	½ cup
	oil for deep frying	

Before using dogfish, the fillets must be premarinated (see index). Remove dogfish fillets from marinade 30 minutes before frying and pat dry with paper towels. Cut into serving-size portions.

Combine 175 mL (¾ cup) flour, 2 mL (½ tsp.) salt and pepper in a clean brown paper bag.

To make batter, beat 175 mL (¾ cup) flour, egg, 2 mL (½ tsp.) salt and water in a bowl until well blended and smooth (or use any other batter recipe in this book, see index).

Dip fillets into bag of seasoned flour and shake until well coated, then dip fish in batter.

Preheat vegetable oil to 180°C (365°F). Deep fry fish for 3 to 5 minutes, depending on the thickness of the fillets. Serves 4.

PAN-FRIED DOGFISH FILLETS

750 g	dogfish fillets	1½ lbs.
2	eggs	2
30 mL	water	2 Tbsp.
500 mL	dry breadcrumbs	2 cups
5 mL	salt	1 tsp.
1 mL	pepper	¼ tsp.
1 mL	orégano	¼ tsp.
1 mL	dill weed	¼ tsp.
	oil for pan frying	

Before using dogfish, the fillets must be premarinated (see index). Remove dogfish fillets from marinade 30 minutes before frying and pat dry with paper towels. Cut into serving-size portions.

To make egg wash, lightly beat eggs with the water in a bowl.

In another bowl, mix together breadcrumbs, salt, pepper, orégano and dill (or use any other breading recipe in this book, see index).

Dip fillets in the egg wash, then into the breadcrumbs, pressing with the fingers to make sure of an even covering.

Heat oil in a skillet and pan fry fillets according to the timing rule (see index). Serves 4.

FILLET OF SOLE BONNE FEMME

1 kg	sole fillets	2 lbs.
250 mL	water	1 cup
250 mL	dry white wine	1 cup
1 small	onion, thinly sliced	1 small
½	lemon, thinly sliced	½
2 mL	salt	½ tsp.
2 mL	peppercorns	½ tsp.
50 mL	butter	¼ cup
250 mL	mushrooms, sliced	1 cup
50 mL	flour	¼ cup
175 mL	light cream	¾ cup
15 mL	lemon juice	1 Tbsp.
	salt and pepper	

Put water, wine, onion, lemon, salt and peppercorns in a large saucepan and bring to a boil. Place fillets in liquid in a single layer (add boiling water to cover, if necessary) and simmer according to the timing rule (see index).

Remove fillets, drain, and place in a lightly greased, shallow baking dish. Strain poaching liquid and return to saucepan. Boil liquid uncovered over high heat until reduced to 175 mL (¾ cup).

In another saucepan, melt butter and sauté mushrooms for 2 to 3 minutes. Add flour, then gradually add strained liquid and cream, stirring over medium heat until thickened. Add lemon juice, salt and pepper; mix well. Pour this sauce over the fillets, covering them completely.

Place the fillets under a preheated broiler 10 to 12 cm (5 to 6″) from heat source and cook for 2 to 3 minutes until the sauce starts to brown. Serves 4.

Options: lake whitefish, pickerel or red snapper

FILLET OF SOLE SUPREME

1 kg	sole fillets	2 lbs.
30 mL	butter	2 Tbsp.
2 mL	salt	½ tsp.
0.5 mL	pepper	⅛ tsp.
4	green onions, thinly sliced	4
	tarragon and chervil, to taste	
250 mL	soft breadcrumbs	1 cup
75 mL	dry vermouth OR white wine	⅓ cup
50 mL	butter	¼ cup

Melt 30 mL (2 Tbsp.) of butter in the bottom of a baking pan. Salt and pepper both sides of fillets and dip them in the melted butter. Spread green onions, tarragon and chervil evenly over bottom of the baking pan which held the butter. Place fillets in a single layer on top of the green onions. Cover with breadcrumbs. Sprinkle with vermouth and dot with 50 mL (¼ cup) butter, cut in small pieces.

Preheat oven to 190°C (375°F) and bake fillets for 15 to 20 minutes until breadcrumbs are browned and fish tests done. Serves 4 to 6.

Options: cod, haddock, cusk, inconnu or pickerel

FISH PIE

500 g	fish fillets	1 lb.
5 mL	salt	1 tsp.
375 mL	boiling water	1½ cups
250 mL	potato, cubed	1 cup
250 mL	carrot, diced	1 cup
250 mL	celery, sliced	1 cup
125 mL	onion, chopped	½ cup
125 mL	green pepper, chopped	½ cup
125 mL	tomato, chopped	½ cup
50 mL	mushrooms, chopped	¼ cup
30 mL	butter	2 Tbsp.
30 mL	flour	2 Tbsp.
5 mL	orégano	1 tsp.
5 mL	salt	1 tsp.
1 mL	pepper	¼ tsp.
1 can	refrigerated biscuits OR	1 can
	pie pastry, enough for 1 crust OR	
500 mL	mashed potato	2 cups

Cut fillets into 2.5 cm (1″) cubes.

Add salt to boiling water, then add potato, carrot, celery, onion and green pepper. Simmer for about 10 minutes until tender-crisp. Drain and reserve broth; if necessary, add water to make 375 mL (1½ cups). Mix together drained vegetables, tomato, mushrooms and fish; place in a lightly greased 2-L (2-qt.) casserole.

Melt butter in a saucepan and blend in flour and orégano. Gradually add reserved broth, stirring over medium heat until thickened. Add salt and pepper. Pour this sauce over the fish and vegetables in the casserole. Open refrigerated biscuits and arrange on top of the casserole. Alternatively, top with pie crust or mashed potato.

Preheat oven to 200°C (400°F) and bake for 20 to 25 minutes or until biscuits are golden. Serves 4 to 6.

Options: cod, halibut, rockfish, haddock or lake whitefish

FISH POACHED IN MILK

500 g	fish fillets, smoked OR unsmoked	1 lb.
2 mL	salt (omit if fish is smoked)	½ tsp.
250 mL	milk	1 cup
30 mL	butter	2 Tbsp.
30 mL	flour	2 Tbsp.
0.5 mL	pepper	⅛ tsp.
5 mL	lemon juice	1 tsp.
30 mL	chives, chopped	2 Tbsp.

Heat salted milk in a shallow pan until almost boiling, then add fish and simmer gently according to the timing rule (see index). Remove from heat. Carefully transfer fish to a heated platter and keep warm. Reserve the milk.

Melt butter in a saucepan, then blend in flour and pepper. Gradually add the reserved milk, stirring over medium heat until thickened. Add lemon juice and half of the chopped chives. Pour this sauce over the fish and sprinkle with the remaining chives. Serves 3.

Options: most white-fleshed fish, smoked or unsmoked (smoked sablefish or Alaska black cod is delicious cooked this way)

HADDOCK AND CUCUMBER MOUSSE (HOT)

500 g	haddock fillets	1 lb.
625 mL	mushrooms, finely sliced	2½ cups
500 mL	cucumber, peeled and diced	2 cups
15 mL	horseradish	1 Tbsp.
5 mL	lemon juice	1 tsp.
5 mL	parsley, minced	1 tsp.
1 mL	chervil	¼ tsp.
1 mL	paprika	¼ tsp.
30 mL	butter	2 Tbsp.
30 mL	flour	2 Tbsp.
175 mL	light cream	¾ cup
2	eggs, lightly beaten	2
2 mL	salt	½ tsp.
0.5 mL	pepper	⅛ tsp.
	olives and parsley	

Remove skin from fish and discard. Grind or coarsely chop fillets. Pat with a paper towel to remove some of the moisture. In a large bowl, put fish, mushrooms, cucumber, horseradish, lemon juice, parsley, chervil and paprika. Blend thoroughly.

Melt butter in a saucepan and stir in flour. Gradually add light cream, stirring constantly over medium heat until smooth and just starting to thicken. Cool this sauce for 2 minutes, then add the eggs and beat well. Add salt and pepper. Pour over the fish and vegetable mixture, then blend well. Pour the mousse into a well-greased oven mold and cover with foil.

Preheat oven to 190°C (375°F) and bake the mousse for 40 minutes. Remove the foil, gently pour off any surplus liquid, and return mousse to the oven without the foil for a further 20 minutes. Remove from the oven and let sit for a few minutes. Place a plate on top of the mold and invert the mousse very, very carefully onto the plate. Garnish with olives and parsley and serve immediately. If desired, serve with lemon sauce (see index). Makes enough for 4.

Options: any firm-fleshed fish such as halibut, cod or turbot

HERB-BAKED FILLETS

500 g	fish fillets	1 lb.
1 mL	salt	¼ tsp.
0.5 mL	pepper	⅛ tsp.
50 mL	onion, chopped	¼ cup
2	tomatoes, sliced	2
2 mL	sweet basil	½ tsp.
30 mL	melted butter	2 Tbsp.

Place fillets in a greased shallow baking dish. Sprinkle fish with salt, pepper and onion. Cover fillets with tomato slices, then sprinkle with sweet basil. Drizzle with melted butter.

Preheat oven to 230°C (450°F) and bake fillets according to the timing rule (see index). Serves 2 to 3.

Options: cod, sole, pickerel, haddock or rockfish

LOBSTER

WHOLE BROILED LOBSTER

Before broiling whole live lobster, place it shell side down, split lengthwise, and remove intestinal veins and stomach. Scoop out the greenish tomalley (liver) and the coral roe (if any); either discard or keep to make tomalley spread and coral roe butter. Place lobster flesh side up on a broiler pan; brush with melted butter and season lightly. Broil 10 cm (4″) from heat for 10 to 12 minutes or until lightly browned. Serve with lemon wedges and melted butter or coral roe butter.

BROILED LOBSTER TAILS

Before broiling lobster tails, use kitchen shears to cut along the underside, clipping off the many legs along the outer edges. Peel off the soft undershell and discard. Bend the tail back to crack some of the joints; this prevents curling. Arrange shell side up on a broiler pan and cook 10 to 12.5 cm (4 to 5″) from heat for 4 minutes. Remove from broiler. Turn tails over, brush with melted butter and season lightly. Broil for another 5 minutes. Serve with lemon wedges and melted butter or coral roe butter.

CORAL ROE BUTTER

50 mL	butter, softened	¼ cup
15 mL	coral roe	1 Tbsp.
5 mL	parsley, minced	1 tsp.
1 mL	salt	¼ tsp.

Mix all ingredients together and chill before serving. Serve on top of broiled or barbecued lobster, fish steaks or fillets.

TOMALLEY SPREAD

30 mL	tomalley	2 Tbsp.
5 mL	mayonnaise	1 tsp.
1 mL	horseradish	¼ tsp.

Blend all ingredients together and serve with crackers as an hors d'oeuvre.

LOBSTER CREPES SUPREME

CREPES

250 mL	flour	1 cup
2	eggs	2
300 mL	milk	1¼ cups
2 mL	salt	½ tsp.

To make crêpes, combine flour, eggs, milk and salt, beating lightly until smooth.

Make crêpes one at a time. Pour 50 mL (3 Tbsp.) batter into a lightly greased, heated frying pan. Tilt pan rapidly so that batter will spread into a thin, even circle about 15 cm (6″) in diameter. Cook until lightly brown, then flip over and brown the other side. Stack crêpes in a pile, using a towel or wax paper between each to keep them separate. Makes about 12 crêpes.

FILLING

500 g	lobster meat	1 lb.
50 mL	butter	¼ cup
50 mL	green onion, chopped	¼ cup
50 mL	green pepper, minced	¼ cup
250 mL	mushrooms, minced	1 cup
50 mL	flour	¼ cup
250 mL	milk	1 cup
50 mL	dry white wine	¼ cup
15 mL	lemon juice	1 Tbsp.
5 mL	salt	1 tsp.
1 mL	pepper	¼ tsp.
2 mL	dried dill weed	½ tsp.

To make the filling for the crêpes, cut or break lobster meat into bite-size pieces.

Melt butter in a saucepan and sauté green onion, green pepper and mushrooms for 2 minutes. Stir in flour, then slowly add milk, stirring constantly over medium heat until thickened. Add wine, lemon juice, salt, pepper, dill and lobster. Remove from heat.

Spoon 50 mL (3 Tbsp.) of this filling onto each crêpe and roll up, folding down the ends so that the filling is contained. Arrange filled crêpes in a lightly greased, shallow oven dish and cover.

Preheat oven to 180°C (350°F) and bake filled crêpes for 10 to 15 minutes until heated through. If desired, heat the remaining filling, thinned as necessary with milk or sour cream, and serve in a separate dish to spoon over the crêpes.

Options: crab, shrimp, oysters, clams, canned salmon or tuna

LOBSTER IN ZUCCHINI BOATS

500 g	cooked lobster meat	1 lb.
4 large	zucchini	4 large
1	egg, lightly beaten	1
30 mL	mayonnaise	2 Tbsp.
50 mL	green onion, minced	¼ cup
50 mL	mozzarella cheese, grated	¼ cup
30 mL	parsley, minced	2 Tbsp.
2 mL	salt	½ tsp.
0.5 mL	pepper	⅛ tsp.
1 mL	orégano	¼ tsp.
30 mL	canned pimento, minced	2 Tbsp.
50 mL	dry breadcrumbs	¼ cup
15 mL	melted butter	1 Tbsp.

Wash zucchini and cut off ends. Cook whole in boiling, salted water for 5 minutes. Cut in half lengthwise and remove pulp from shells, leaving a complete boat. Chop the pulp finely and mix with all the remaining ingredients—except breadcrumbs and melted butter. Pile this mixture into the zucchini boats and place them on a lightly greased baking dish. Combine breadcrumbs with melted butter, then sprinkle on top of the filled boats.

Preheat oven to 180°C (350°F) and bake for 20 to 25 minutes or until lightly browned. If using as an appetizer, cut each boat in two and serve with a wedge of lemon. As a main course, each person may be offered two boats. Serves 16 as an appetizer, 4 as a main course.

Options: shrimp, crab or scallops

MUSTARD-BROILED MACKEREL

2 1-kg	whole mackerel	2 2-lb.
15 mL	parsley, chopped	1 Tbsp.
5 mL	salt	1 tsp.
a few grains	pepper	a few grains
30 mL	melted butter	2 Tbsp.
5 mL	prepared mustard	1 tsp.
0.5 mL	dried dill weed	⅛ tsp.
15 mL	lemon juice	1 Tbsp.
	lemon wedges	

If not already dressed, clean and scale mackerel. Bone and fillet the fish, then rinse under cold running water and pat dry with paper towels. Place fillets skin side down on a greased broiler pan.

In a small bowl, blend parsley, salt and pepper with 15 mL (1 Tbsp.) of the melted butter. Brush fillets well with this mixture before broiling 7.5 cm (3″) from source of heat for about 5 minutes. Remove from heat, leaving broiler on.

Blend remaining butter in a small bowl with mustard, dill and lemon juice. Pour this over the fillets and broil for 5 more minutes. Garnish with lemon wedges. Serves 4.

Options: herring, alewife, tuna or tullibee

Ocean Perch Citrus Fillets

500 g	ocean perch fillets	1 lb.
50 mL	melted butter	¼ cup
15 mL	orange OR lemon juice	1 Tbsp.
5 mL	salt	1 tsp.
1 mL	fennel	¼ tsp.
15 mL	orange OR lemon rind, coarsely grated	1 Tbsp.
6 slices	orange OR lemon	6 slices
	parsley	

Place fillets skin side down in a well greased, shallow baking dish. In a bowl, combine melted butter, orange juice, salt and fennel. Pour over the fillets. Sprinkle fish with grated orange rind.

Preheat oven to 230°C (450°F) and bake fish according to the timing rule (see index). Garnish with orange slices and parsley. Serves 2 to 3.

Pacific Salmon Wellington

1 kg	salmon fillets	2 lbs.
75 mL	whipping cream	⅓ cup
2 mL	salt	½ tsp.
0.5 mL	pepper	⅛ tsp.

Divide salmon into two portions of 750 and 250 g (1½ and ½ lb.). Put the smaller portion through a meat grinder or chop finely, then blend with whipping cream, salt and pepper. Cut the larger portion into very thin slices.

15 mL	butter	1 Tbsp.
125 mL	onion, minced	½ cup

Melt butter in a frying pan and sauté onion until soft but not brown. Remove from heat and set aside.

15 mL	flour	1 Tbsp.
15 mL	unsalted butter, softened	1 Tbsp.
1 mL	salt	¼ tsp.
pinch	pepper, freshly ground	pinch

Prepare beurre manié by combining flour, butter, salt and pepper. Blend well.

15 mL	butter	1 Tbsp.
125 mL	mushrooms, sliced	½ cup
125 mL	whipping cream	½ cup
10 mL	lemon juice	2 tsp.
	salt and pepper	

Melt butter in a frying pan and sauté mushrooms. Add whipping cream and cook over medium heat, stirring constantly, until the liquid is reduced by half. Stir in the beurre manié and simmer for 5 minutes. Add lemon juice. Season with salt and pepper to taste. Remove from heat and set aside.

2 215-g pkgs.	puff pastry, enough for a 2-crust pie	2 7-oz. pkgs.
5	hard-cooked eggs, halved lengthwise	5
1	egg, beaten	1

Roll out puff pastry into two pieces, each 30 × 15 cm (12 × 6″). Place one piece on a buttered baking sheet. Along the centre of the pastry, arrange a layer of half the salmon slices. Top with the sautéed onions, then with half of the mushroom mixture. Cover with remaining salmon slices. Top with two rows of hard-cooked egg halves. Spread with remaining mushroom mixture. Cover with minced salmon mixture.

Place the second piece of pastry over the layers, brush the edges with beaten egg, and seal well. Brush the top of the pastry with beaten egg and use a fork to punch several holes in the pastry in a decorative pattern.

Preheat oven to 200°C (400°F) and bake for 25 minutes. Make sherry-mushroom cream sauce (see index) to accompany this dish. Serves 8 to 10.

PAELLA VALENCIA

250 g	sweet Spanish OR Italian spiced sausage	½ lb.
12 small	clams in the shell	12 small
12	mussels in the shell	12
50 mL	olive oil	¼ cup
8 pieces	chicken, drumsticks and thighs	8 pieces
1 large	onion, coarsely chopped	1 large
1 clove	garlic, minced	1 clove
2	tomatoes, peeled, seeded and diced	2
30 mL	canned pimento, chopped	2 Tbsp.
5 mL	salt	1 tsp.
1 mL	paprika	¼ tsp.
1 mL	saffron	¼ tsp.
375 mL	long-grain rice	1½ cups
280 g	peas	10 oz.
500 g	green beans	1 lb.
750 mL	dry white wine	3 cups
1.5 kg	large shrimp, shelled and deveined	3 lbs.

Poach sausage in water for about 15 minutes until cooked. Remove, cool and cut into slices.

Steam clams and mussels until the shells open. Drain, reserving 250 mL (1 cup) of liquid.

Heat olive oil in a large skillet and cook chicken over medium heat, turning to brown on all sides. Remove chicken. Sauté onion and garlic in drippings until translucent. Add tomatoes, pimento, salt, paprika and saffron, then stir over medium heat for one more minute. Add rice and stir until coated with oil. Add peas and green beans; stir to mix. Pour this mixture into a 4-L (4-qt.) paella pan or casserole dish. Pour wine and reserved liquid over the rice and vegetable mixture. Arrange shrimp, sausage and chicken over the rice and vegetables.

Preheat oven to 175°C (350°F) and bake paella, covered, for about one hour. Remove and fluff up rice with a fork. Place clams and mussels on top, cover, and return to oven for another 10 minutes. Serve from the casserole dish. Makes enough for 8.

POLYNESIAN FILLETS

1 kg	fish fillets	2 lbs.
15 mL	butter	1 Tbsp.
5 mL	salt	1 tsp.
dash	pepper	dash
50 mL	lemon juice	¼ cup
15 mL	cornstarch	1 Tbsp.
125 mL	chicken bouillon OR broth	½ cup
30 mL	butter	2 Tbsp.
250 mL	celery, diagonally sliced	1 cup
125 mL	green pepper, thinly sliced	½ cup
5 mL	ginger, minced	1 tsp.
250 mL	fresh bean sprouts OR	1 cup
450-mL can	bean sprouts, drained	15-oz. can
15 mL	soy sauce	1 Tbsp.
15 mL	molasses	1 Tbsp.
50 mL	concentrated orange juice	¼ cup
15 mL	orange rind, grated	1 Tbsp.

Arrange fillets on greased aluminum foil on a baking sheet. Dot fish with 15 mL (1 Tbsp.) butter and season with salt, pepper and lemon juice.

Preheat oven to 230°C (450°F) and bake according to the timing rule (see index). Transfer fish to a serving dish and keep warm.

Soften cornstarch with 30 mL (2 Tbsp.) of the chicken bouillon.

Melt 30 mL (2 Tbsp.) butter in a saucepan and sauté celery, green pepper and ginger until tender. Add bean sprouts, soy sauce, molasses, rest of chicken bouillon and orange juice. Heat until almost boiling. Add cornstarch mixture and stir over medium heat until thick and clear. Spoon over the fillets and sprinkle with orange rind. Serves 6.

Options: cod, red snapper, sole, pickerel or turbot

RED SNAPPER AND CHEESE SOUFFLE

500 g	steamed red snapper, flaked	1 lb.
30 mL	onion, minced	2 Tbsp.
15 mL	parsley, minced	1 Tbsp.
8 slices	buttered bread, cut in cubes	8 slices
250 mL	cheddar cheese, grated	1 cup
3	eggs, slightly beaten	3
425 mL	milk	1¾ cups
2 mL	Worcestershire sauce	½ tsp.
15 mL	lemon juice	1 Tbsp.
2 drops	Tabasco sauce	2 drops
5 mL	salt	1 tsp.
0.5 mL	white pepper	⅛ tsp.

Toss flaked fish with onion and parsley. In a blender, put half of each of the following: bread cubes, cheese, fish mixture, eggs and milk. Turn on high until thoroughly mixed. Empty into a bowl.

Repeat this step in the blender with the remaining ingredients. Combine this with the first mixture and pour into a greased casserole or soufflé dish.

Preheat oven to 180°C (350°F) and bake soufflé for one hour or until set in the centre. Serves 3 to 4.

Options: any white-fleshed fish such as rockfish, pollock (Boston bluefish), turbot, pickerel or carp

ROAST MACKEREL WITH WINE SAUCE

3 large OR	mackerel, dressed	3 large OR
6 small	and boned	6 small
	lemon juice	
	salt and pepper	
50 mL	butter	¼ cup
125 mL	onion, chopped	½ cup
1 clove	garlic, crushed	1 clove
500 mL	mushrooms, sliced	2 cups

15 mL	flour	1 Tbsp.
2 mL	salt	½ tsp.
125 mL	dry white wine	½ cup
125 mL	chicken bouillon OR broth	½ cup

Season mackerel cavities with salt and pepper, then place each fish, cavity down, on a rack in a baking pan. Sprinkle the outside of fish with lemon juice, salt and pepper.

Preheat oven to 230°C (450°F) and bake fish according to the timing rule (see index). Remove from oven, skin, and place on a serving dish. Keep warm while preparing the sauce.

In a saucepan, melt butter and sauté onion and garlic until onion is translucent. Add mushrooms and sauté for a further 2 minutes. Blend in flour and salt, then gradually add wine and chicken bouillon, stirring over medium heat until thickened. Pour sauce over fish and serve. Makes enough for 6.

Options: herring, alewife or shad

SALMON STEAKS ORIENTAL

6	salmon steaks OR fillets, 3.75 cm (1½″) thick	6
125 mL	Japanese soy sauce	½ cup
50 mL	brown sugar	¼ cup
250 mL	apéritif wine, such as Dubonnet OR St. Raphael	1 cup

Blend soy sauce, sugar and wine in a large, flat dish. Place salmon in this marinade for at least one hour, turning occasionally. The fish may be barbecued (see index) or broiled.

To barbecue, arrange the salmon in a greased basket grill and broil about 10 cm (4″) above hot coals. Turn 2 or 3 times, brushing with the marinade each time. Cook for about 7 minutes each side or until flesh is opaque and milky through to the centre.

To broil, preheat broiler for 5 minutes. Place fish 10 to 12.5 cm (4 to 5″) from heat and cook for 5 to 7 minutes. Turn, brush with the marinade and cook for a further 5 to 7 minutes. Serves 6.

Options: trout or arctic charr

Seafood Kabobs

500 g	seafood	1 lb.
12 pieces	green pepper, cut into	12 pieces
	3.75 cm (1½″) squares OR	
12 slices	zucchini, 5 mm (¼″) thick	12 slices
12	cherry tomatoes	12
12	mushroom caps	12
3 slices	bacon, cut into quarters	3 slices
50 mL	lemon juice	¼ cup
50 mL	melted butter	¼ cup
	salt and pepper	
	hot cooked rice	

Blanch all crisp vegetables such as green pepper, mushrooms and zucchini pieces in boiling water for one minute to prevent them from splitting and falling off skewers.

Cut fillets into 3.75 cm (1½″) cubes. Cut small whole fish such as smelt in half across the width. Alternate seafood with the vegetables and bacon on well-greased skewers.

Mix melted butter and lemon juice in a bowl. Brush this mixture over each filled skewer, then sprinkle with salt and pepper. Place filled skewers on a foil-lined pan and broil 7.5 to 10 cm (3 to 4″) from heat (or on a barbecue grill) for 10 to 12 minutes, turning once or twice to ensure even cooking. Serve over hot cooked rice. Makes 3 to 4 servings.

Options: oysters, shrimp, crab legs, smelt; salmon, halibut or other white-fleshed fish

SKATE BEURRE NOIR

500 g	skate wings	1 lb.
1 L	water	1 qt.
50 mL	cider OR wine vinegar	3 Tbsp.
5 mL	salt	1 tsp.

If the wings are large, cut them into serving-size pieces; otherwise, leave whole.

In a large saucepan, combine water, vinegar and salt. Add more water if necessary to cover the wings. Bring this liquid to a boil. Place the wings in the liquid and poach them, simmering, according to the timing rule (see index). Transfer fish to a serving dish and keep warm.

BEURRE NOIR SAUCE

50 mL	butter	¼ cup
10 mL	cider OR wine vinegar OR lemon juice	2 tsp.
30 mL	capers OR parsley, chopped	2 Tbsp.
	salt and pepper	

In a small saucepan, melt butter over medium heat until golden brown. Add vinegar and capers (or lemon juice and parsley), stirring to blend well. Season with salt and pepper. While sauce is very hot, spoon it over the fish and serve immediately. Serves 2.

STIR-FRIED SQUID, CHINESE STYLE

750 g	squid tubes	1½ lbs.
30 mL	oil	2 Tbsp.
1 clove	garlic, crushed	1 clove
10 mL	ginger, minced	2 tsp.
1 small	onion, thinly sliced	1 small
250 mL	mushrooms, sliced	1 cup
250 mL	celery, sliced	1 cup
125 mL	green pepper, thinly sliced	½ cup
15 mL	cornstarch	1 Tbsp.
30 mL	soy sauce	2 Tbsp.
5 mL	sugar	1 tsp.
5 mL	white vinegar	1 tsp.
175 mL	beef bouillon OR broth	¾ cup
5 mL	salt	1 tsp.
1 mL	pepper	¼ tsp.

Simmer squid tubes in enough boiling, salted water to cover for one hour, or pressure cook for 5 minutes. Cut into thin strips.

Heat oil in a wok or large frying pan and add garlic, ginger, onion, mushrooms, celery and green pepper. Stir fry for 3 minutes over high heat. Add squid and stir fry for 2 to 3 minutes longer.

In a bowl, blend together remaining ingredients, then add to squid mixture, stirring over medium heat until the sauce thickens. Serves 4.

Options: salmon, halibut, cusk or turbot, cut into 2.5 cm (1″) cubes; oysters, crab legs, lobster, shrimp or scallops, cut into bite-size pieces. Toss fish or shellfish raw into stir-fried vegetables and cook for 3 to 4 minutes longer, then continue with recipe.

STUFFED FILLET ROLLS

1 kg	fish fillets	2 lbs.
5 mL	salt	1 tsp.
1 mL	pepper	¼ tsp.
	stuffing (see index)	
30 mL	melted butter	2 Tbsp.
2 slices	bacon, cut in squares	2 slices

Sprinkle fillets with salt and pepper. Make stuffed rolls by one of the following two methods:

1. Spread a layer of stuffing over each fillet and roll up, securing with a toothpick. Place rolls in a well greased, shallow baking pan. Brush tops with melted butter and scatter bacon pieces over the top.

2. Line cups in a greased muffin tin with fillets, overlapping the ends. Place stuffing in centre of each cup. Brush tops with melted butter and place a piece of bacon in the centre of each cup.

Preheat oven to 230°C (450°F) and bake for 15 to 20 minutes. Serve as is or with a cream sauce (see index). Makes 4 to 6 servings.

Options: sole, redfish (ocean perch) or pickerel

SWORDFISH STROGANOFF

750 g	swordfish steaks	1½ lbs.
1 L	water	1 qt.
30 mL	lemon juice	2 Tbsp.
50 mL	butter	¼ cup
250 mL	onion, chopped	1 cup
250 mL	mushrooms, sliced	1 cup
15 mL	butter	1 Tbsp.
375 mL	sour cream	1½ cups
50 mL	dry white wine	¼ cup
10 mL	lemon juice	2 tsp.
5 mL	prepared mustard	1 tsp.
1 mL	sweet basil	¼ tsp.
2 mL	salt	½ tsp.
1 mL	pepper	¼ tsp.
1 L	cooked green noodles, hot and buttered	1 qt.
	paprika, parsley and lemon wedges	

Cut fish into strips 1 × 5 cm (½ × 2″). Marinate for 3 to 4 hours in water and 30 mL (2 Tbsp.) lemon juice, adding more water if necessary to cover fish.

In a skillet, melt 50 mL (¼ cup) butter and sauté onion until translucent and tender. Add mushrooms and sauté another 2 to 3 minutes. Remove onion and mushrooms from pan. Add 15 mL (1 Tbsp.) butter, then sauté the fish strips, turning occasionaly, for 3 to 4 minutes. Remove fish and keep warm.

In a saucepan, blend sour cream, wine, lemon juice, mustard, basil, salt and pepper, over medium heat. Stir in onions and mushrooms and heat until almost boiling. Carefully stir in the fish strips; heat but do not boil. Serve immediately over hot noodles, garnished with paprika, parsley and lemon wedges. Makes 4 servings.

TUNA

Fresh or frozen tuna steaks or small whole tuna may be cooked a number of ways. Allow 125 g (8 oz.) per person.

BAKED WHOLE TUNA

1 whole	tuna	1 whole
1 L	cold water	1 qt.
125 mL	white vinegar	½ cup
30 to 50 mL	lemon juice	2 to 3 Tbsp.
5 mL	salt	1 tsp.
1 mL	pepper	¼ tsp.
5 mL	rosemary	1 tsp.
5 mL	sweet basil	1 tsp.
30 mL	melted butter	2 Tbsp.
	lemon wedges	

If not already dressed, clean tuna (see index). Mix water with vinegar, then wipe the fish with a cloth wrung out in this solution. Rinse out any blood from the cavity.

Place the fish on a rack in a baking pan, cavity down, and bake in an oven preheated to 180°C (350°F) for 20 minutes. Remove fish from oven, leaving oven on.

Take off skin and fat from the outside of the tuna and discard. Split the fish from head to tail and remove the backbone. Season inside and out with lemon juice, salt, pepper, rosemary and basil, then drizzle with melted butter. Carefully replace one fillet on top of the other and return to the oven. Continue baking until the fish is tender, allowing about 15 minutes per 500 g (1 lb.). Garnish with lemon wedges. Baked tuna is delicious served with sherry-mushroom cream sauce (see index) or a sauce of your choice.

POACHED TUNA

Albacore steaks, chunks or small whole tuna are excellent poached. Use enough court bouillon (see index) to cover, then poach for about 15 minutes per 2.5 cm (1″) of thickness until the fish flakes easily when tested. Serve with lemon sauce (see index) or other favourite sauce.

SAUTEED TUNA STEAKS

One serving-size albacore steak 2.5 cm (1″) thick per person

150 mL	dry white wine	⅔ cup
5 mL	tarragon	1 tsp.
75 mL	butter	⅓ cup

Blend wine and tarragon and let sit. Melt butter in a skillet, add steak and brown on both sides. Spoon the tarragon wine over the fish as it cooks. Steaks will be done in 10 to 15 minutes, depending on thickness. When done, remove fish to a serving platter and pour the remaining tarragon wine over it.

TURBOT CREOLE

1 kg	turbot fillets	2 lbs.
30 mL	butter	2 Tbsp.
30 mL	onion, chopped	2 Tbsp.
50 mL	green pepper, minced	¼ cup
50 mL	celery, sliced	¼ cup
375 mL	tomato, sliced	1½ cups
50 mL	mushrooms, sliced	¼ cup
50 mL	black pitted olives, sliced	¼ cup
5 mL	salt	1 tsp.
0.5 mL	pepper	⅛ tsp.
1 mL	rosemary	¼ tsp.
30 mL	medium-dry sherry	2 Tbsp.

Arrange fish fillets in a greased baking dish.

In a saucepan, melt butter and sauté onion, green pepper and celery until tender. Add tomato, mushrooms and olives, then cook for 2 minutes more. Add salt, pepper, rosemary and sherry, stirring to blend. Pour over fillets.

Preheat oven to 230°C (450°F) and bake fish for 10 to 15 minutes, depending on thickness of fillets. Serves 6.

Options: any other white-fleshed fish such as red snapper, wolffish, cusk, inconnu, cod or haddock

WHOLE STUFFED SALMON

3 kg	whole salmon	6.5 lbs.
5 mL	seasoned salt	1 tsp.
1 mL	pepper	¼ tsp.
375 to 500 mL	stuffing (see index)	1½ to 2 cups
30 mL	melted butter OR oil	2 Tbsp.

If not already dressed, clean and scale the salmon, removing bones if desired (see index for techniques). A boned fish allows for easier serving and more pleasant eating.

Sprinkle the cavity of the fish with seasoned salt and pepper. Fill cavity with stuffing. Secure the edges of the salmon with turkey skewers and lace up with string. Brush outside of the salmon with melted butter. May be baked in the oven or barbecued.

Preheat the oven to 230°C (450°F) and bake according to the timing rule (see index). A 3-kg (6.5-lb.) stuffed fish will measure 6 to 7.5 cm (2½ to 3″) through the thickest part and will take no longer than 30 minutes.

See index for barbecuing directions. With the correct conditions, a 3-kg (6.5-lb.) stuffed fish will require 15 to 20 minutes on each side, turning only once mid-way through cooking. Serves about 12 people.

Options: lake whitefish, trout or arctic charr

✎Sandwiches✎

Bombay Shrimp Sandwiches

500 g	cooked tiny shrimp OR	1 lb.
4 113-g cans	shrimp	4 4-oz. cans
15 mL	lemon juice	1 Tbsp
2 mL	curry powder	½ tsp.
1 small	apple, finely diced	1 small
125 mL	mayonnaise (or to taste)	½ cup
2 mL	salt	½ tsp.
0.5 mL	pepper	⅛ tsp.

If using canned shrimp, drain, rinse under cold running water, and drain again. Mix all ingredients together and blend well. Chill for 30 minutes before serving. Good when served on rye or wholewheat bread. Makes 6 to 8 sandwiches.

Options: fresh or canned crab, or canned tuna

CLAMBURGERS

500 g	cooked OR canned clams, drained and minced	1 lb.
2	eggs	2
30 mL	lemon juice	2 Tbsp.
30 mL	green onion, minced	2 Tbsp.
30 mL	parsley, minced	2 Tbsp.
150 mL	dry breadcrumbs	⅔ cup
2 mL	salt	½ tsp.
few grains	pepper	few grains
30 to 50 mL	oil	2 to 3 Tbsp.
4	hamburger buns	4
	butter	
	ketchup OR tartare sauce (see index)	

Beat eggs lightly, then add clams, lemon juice, green onion, parsley, breadcrumbs, salt and pepper. Mix well, then shape into 4 patties.

Preheat oil in a skillet and pan fry patties, turning once, until nicely browned on both sides.

Split buns and toast lightly, then butter. Place a clam patty between the halves. Serve with ketchup or tartare sauce. Makes 4 clamburgers.

Options: canned salmon or tuna

FILLET AND ANCHOVY SANDWICHES

250 mL	cooked fish fillets, flaked	1 cup
50-g can	anchovies, drained and well mashed	2-oz. can
30 mL	green onion, chopped	2 Tbsp.
15 mL	lemon juice	1 Tbsp.
30 mL	sour cream	2 Tbsp.

Combine all ingredients and blend well. Good served on plain or toasted bread. Makes 3 sandwiches.

Options: red snapper, sole, cod, turbot or pickerel

FILLET AND OLIVE SANDWICHES

500 mL	cooked fish fillets, flaked	2 cups
30 mL	lemon juice	2 Tbsp.
125 mL	green olives, chopped	½ cup
125 mL	mayonnaise	½ cup
	salt and pepper to taste	

Combine all ingredients and blend well. Very tasty on plain or toasted bread. Makes 8 sandwiches.

Options: any firm, white-fleshed fish

HOT OPEN-FACED SHRIMP RAREBIT

112 g	cooked shrimp OR	4 oz.
113-g can	tiny shrimp	4-oz. can
4 slices	bread OR	4 slices
2	kaiser rolls, halved	2
	butter	
250 mL	medium cheddar cheese, grated	1 cup
1	egg, lightly beaten	1
1 mL	Worcestershire sauce	¼ tsp.
2 mL	dry mustard	½ tsp.
2 mL	vinegar	½ tsp.
	salt and pepper to taste	

If using canned shrimp, drain, rinse under cold running water, and drain again.

Toast bread slices lightly on both sides and butter.

Chop shrimp coarsely and combine with the rest of the ingredients. Spread in equal portions on each slice of toast. These sandwiches may be baked or broiled.

To bake, preheat oven to 200°C (400°F) and cook for 5 minutes. To broil, place 12.5 cm (5″) from heat and cook for 3 to 5 minutes. Serves 2 to 4.

PAN-GRILLED INCONNU SANDWICHES

250 mL	cooked inconnu fillets, flaked	1 cup
75 mL	mayonnaise	⅓ cup
30 mL	onion, minced	2 Tbsp.
5 mL	lemon juice	1 tsp.
1 mL	Worcestershire sauce	¼ tsp.
1 mL	salt	¼ tsp.
6 slices	bread	6 slices
	butter, softened	

Blend together all the ingredients—except bread and butter—and mix well. Spread filling on 3 lightly buttered slices of bread and top with remaining slices. Trim crusts if desired.

Spread the outside of the sandwiches with butter and brown both sides in a hot frying pan. Makes 3 sandwiches.

Options: most other white-fleshed fish

SALMON FRENCH TOAST SANDWICHES

250 g	cooked salmon, flaked OR	1 cup
220-g can	salmon	7.75-oz. can
50 mL	mayonnaise	¼ cup
15 mL	parsley, chopped	1 Tbsp.
30 mL	green onion, minced	2 Tbsp.
2 mL	salt	½ tsp.
0.5 mL	pepper	⅛ tsp.
2 drops	Tabasco sauce	2 drops
8 slices	bread, buttered	8 slices
1	egg, beaten	1
125 mL	milk (and salmon liquid, if any)	½ cup
30 to 50 mL	butter	2 to 3 Tbsp.

If using canned salmon, drain and reserve juice.

Flake salmon (mashing bones and skin if canned). Mix well with mayonnaise, parsley, green onion, salt, pepper and Tabasco. Spread this filling on 4 slices of the buttered bread and top with remaining slices.

In a shallow bowl, combine egg and milk (including salmon juice, if any). Dip both sides of each sandwich into this mixture.

Melt butter in a frying pan and brown both sides of each sandwich. Serve immediately. Makes 4 sandwiches.

Option: canned tuna

SALMON SCRAMBLE ON A BUN

250 mL	cooked salmon OR	1 cup
220-g can	salmon	7.75-oz. can
3	eggs, lightly beaten	3
5 mL	butter	1 tsp.
2 mL	salt	½ tsp.
0.5 mL	pepper	⅛ tsp.
0.5 mL	tarragon	⅛ tsp.
0.5 mL	basil	⅛ tsp.
50 mL	French dressing (see index) OR prepared French dressing	¼ cup
30 mL	green onion, chopped	2 Tbsp.
6	hamburger buns	6
125 mL	Swiss or cheddar cheese, grated	½ cup

If using canned salmon, drain liquid into a bowl, add eggs and beat well. If using fresh salmon, beat eggs with 15 mL (1 Tbsp.) cold water.

Melt butter in frying pan and scramble the eggs. Remove from heat. Add salmon, salt, pepper, tarragon, basil, French dressing and green onions. Mix well.

Cut hamburger buns in half and toast lightly, then divide the salmon mixture evenly among the bottom halves of the buns. Top with cheese, then place the tops on the buns. Wrap buns separately in heavy-duty foil.

Buns may be baked in the oven or barbecued. To bake, cook in oven preheated to 180°C (350°F) for 15 minutes. To barbecue, place on grill for about 15 minutes until heated through and the cheese melts. Makes 6 servings.

SEAFOOD BURGERS

500 g	seafood	1 lb.
	breading (see index)	
	butter	
8	kaiser rolls OR hamburger buns	8
8 slices	cheese	8 slices
8 slices	tomato	8 slices
	lettuce	
	tartare sauce (see index)	

Bread seafood. Melt butter and pan fry seafood until golden brown on all sides.

Cut rolls in half, toast lightly, and butter. On the bottom half of each roll, place a portion of fried seafood, cheese, tomato, lettuce, and a spoonful of tartare sauce. Top with the other half of the roll. Makes 8 seafood burgers.

Options: fillets of cod, sole or red snapper; oysters or clams

SEAFOOD DELUXE SANDWICHES

250 mL	canned seafood	1 cup
2	hard-cooked eggs, chopped	2
125 mL	celery, minced	½ cup
50 mL	stuffed olives, chopped	¼ cup
30 mL	sweet pickle relish	2 Tbsp.
10 mL	prepared mustard	2 tsp.
125 mL	mayonnaise (or to taste)	½ cup
	salt and pepper	
10	slices bread, buttered	10 slices

Drain canned seafood and discard liquid. Flake seafood (mashing bones and skin if using canned salmon). Combine all ingredients—except buttered bread—and season with salt and pepper to taste. Makes 5 sandwiches.

Options: canned salmon, tuna, shrimp, crab or mackerel

SHRIMP AND AVOCADO SANDWICHES

125 g	cooked shrimp	4 oz.
1 small	avocado, peeled and diced	1 small
15 mL	lemon juice	1 Tbsp.
30 mL	mayonnaise	2 Tbsp.
1 mL	dried dill weed	¼ tsp.
	salt and pepper to taste	
6 slices	rye bread, buttered	6 slices

Combine all ingredients—except the buttered bread—and chill for 30 minutes. Makes 3 sandwiches.

Option: canned tuna

TUNA BUNWICHES

184-g can	flaked albacore tuna, drained	6.5-oz. can
6 to 8	hot dog buns	6 to 8
125 mL	medium cheddar cheese, diced	½ cup
2	hard-cooked eggs, chopped	2
50 mL	celery, minced	¼ cup
15 mL	green onion, minced	1 Tbsp.
15 mL	sweet pickle relish	1 Tbsp.
15 mL	pimento, chopped	1 Tbsp.
125 mL	mayonnaise	½ cup
15 mL	lemon juice	1 Tbsp.
	salt and pepper to taste	

Slice hot dog buns in half lengthwise and scoop out the soft centres, leaving about 1.25 cm (½″).

Combine the rest of the ingredients and mix well. Spoon this filling into the bottom halves of the buns, then top with the other halves. Wrap each filled bun in aluminum foil.

Preheat oven to 160°C (325°F) and bake bunwiches for 15 to 20 minutes.

Options: canned salmon, shrimp, crab or mackerel

✿MARINADES✿

HERB AND WINE MARINADE

50 mL	olive oil	¼ cup
5 mL	rosemary OR orégano	1 tsp.
125 mL	tomato, peeled, seeded and diced	½ cup
15 mL	lemon juice	1 Tbsp.
250 mL	dry white wine	1 cup
2 mL	salt	½ tsp.
0.5 mL	pepper	⅛ tsp.

Combine all ingredients and use as a marinade or a sauce for salmon, arctic charr, trout, lake whitefish or most other firm-fleshed fish.

LEMON MARINADE

	juice of one lemon	
1 clove	garlic, minced	1 clove
50 mL	melted butter	¼ cup
2 mL	salt	½ tsp.
1 mL	pepper	¼ tsp.

Combine all ingredients and use as a marinade. May also be brushed on fillets while cooking.

⚙COURT BOUILLONS⚙

To poach fish in a court bouillon, bring the liquid to boil, add fish—the liquid should just cover it—and simmer gently according to the timing rule (see index). A court bouillon may also be used as the liquid in a sauce served with or over the poached fish. The recipes given below can be added to and adapted to suit individual tastes. Court bouillon liquid may be stored in the refrigerator for up to one week or kept frozen for 2 to 3 months.

VINEGAR COURT BOUILLON

30 mL	butter	2 Tbsp.
1	onion, coarsely chopped	1
1	carrot, coarsely chopped	1
1 stalk	celery, coarsely chopped	1 stalk
1.25 L	water	5 cups
50 mL	vinegar	¼ cup
1	bay leaf	1
5 mL	salt	1 tsp.
2 mL	peppercorns	½ tsp.

Melt butter in a large pot and sauté onion, carrot and celery for 5 minutes until golden brown. Add water, vinegar, bay leaf, salt and peppercorns, then simmer, covered, for 30 minutes. Strain and set aside until ready to use.

WINE COURT BOUILLON

500 mL	dry white wine	2 cups
750 mL	water	3 cups
1 small	onion, thinly sliced	1 small
1 small	lemon, thinly sliced	1 small
2 stalks	celery, tops only	2 stalks
	few sprigs parsley	
1	bay leaf	1
5 mL	salt	1 tsp.
2 mL	peppercorns	½ tsp.

Place all ingredients in a large pot and simmer, covered, for 30 minutes. Strain and set aside until ready to use.

BREADINGS AND
✎BATTERS✎

BREADINGS

Before breading, fish fillets and
shellfish should be rinsed, patted dry, and dipped in an egg wash consisting
of one well-beaten egg plus 15 mL (1 Tbsp.) milk or water, or dipped in a
thin batter:

250 mL	flour	1 cup
2 mL	salt	½ tsp.
1	egg	1
375 mL	milk OR water	1½ cups

Mix flour and salt together. In another
bowl, lightly beat egg with milk or water. Pour liquid mixture into dry
mixture and beat until smooth.

After dipping in an egg wash or thin batter, fish fillets or shellfish are
ready to be rolled in one of the following breading variations:

Cornmeal. See recipe for golden pan-fried rainbow trout.
Curry. Mix 250 mL (1 cup) breadcrumbs with 5 mL (1 tsp.) curry
   powder.
Ginger. Mix 250 mL (1 cup) breadcrumbs with 5 mL (1 tsp.) ginger
   powder.
Herb. Mix 250 mL (1 cup) breadcrumbs with one of the following: 5 mL
   (1 tsp.) dried dill weed, fennel, tarragon or chervil.
Nut. Use 250 mL (1 cup) finely chopped nuts.
Onion. Mix 250 mL (1 cup) breadcrumbs with 5 mL (1 tsp.) dried onion
   flakes.

Potato chip. Use 250 mL (1 cup) crushed potato chips.

Parmesan-breadcrumb. Mix 125 mL (½ cup) breadcrumbs with 125 mL (½ cup) grated Parmesan cheese.

Parmesan-cracker. Mix 125 mL (½ cup) crushed crackers with 125 mL (½ cup) grated Parmesan cheese.

BATTERS

Rinse fish or seafood and pat dry before dipping in batter. As a general rule, a batter made with water will be crisp, while a batter made with milk will be tender. Dip cubes of halibut, cod, salmon, trout or other firm-fleshed fish or shellfish into batter and deep fry in oil preheated to 190°C (375°F) for 4 to 5 minutes until golden brown. Drain on absorbent paper. Serve hot with chutney, Richelieu or tartare sauce as dip if desired. (See index for these sauce recipes.)

BASIC TENDER BATTER

375 mL	all-purpose flour	1½ cups
5 mL	baking powder	1 tsp.
5 mL	salt	1 tsp.
2	eggs	2
300 mL	milk	1¼ cups
15 mL	vegetable oil	1 Tbsp.
15 mL	vinegar	1 Tbsp.

Mix all dry ingredients in one bowl, and liquids in another. Pour liquids into dry ingredients and beat until smooth. Allow to stand for 10 minutes before using. Makes enough for 1 to 1.5 kg (2 to 3 lbs.).

CAMPER'S BATTER

| 250 mL | pancake mix | 1 cup |
| 175 mL | beer | ¾ cup |

Combine pancake mix with beer, stirring only until blended. Makes enough batter for about 1 kg (2 lbs.).

CRISPY BATTER

250 mL	all-purpose flour	1 cup
10 mL	baking powder	2 tsp.
7 mL	salt	1½ tsp.
10 mL	sugar	2 tsp.
15 mL	salad oil	1 Tbsp.
250 mL	water	1 cup

Mix dry ingredients well in a bowl. In another bowl, add oil to water, then pour into a well in the dry ingredients. Beat until well blended and smooth. Makes enough for 1 kg (2 lbs.).

HERB BATTER

150 mL	all-purpose flour	¾ cup
5 mL	baking powder	1 tsp.
2 mL	salt	½ tsp.
1 to 2 mL	dried dill weed OR herb of choice	¼ to ½ tsp.
1	egg, lightly beaten	1
100 mL	water OR milk OR flat beer	½ cup

Mix dry ingredients well. Pour egg and water into a well in the dry mix and beat until well blended. Makes enough for 0.5 to 1 kg (1 to 2 lbs.).

LEMON BATTER

250 mL	all-purpose flour	1 cup
5 mL	baking powder	1 tsp.
2 mL	salt	½ tsp.
1	egg, well beaten	1
175 mL	cold water	¾ cup
200 mL	juice of 1 lemon and water	1 scant cup

Sift dry ingredients into a bowl. Make a well in the centre of dry ingredients and add egg and liquids. Beat until smooth. Makes enough for 1 kg (2 lbs.).

WATCHMAN'S BATTER

250 mL	flour	1 cup
250 mL	ice water	1 cup
1 mL	baking soda	¼ tsp.
5 mL	salt	1 tsp.
2 mL	baking powder	½ tsp.

Place flour in a bowl, add water, and beat well. Add the baking soda and salt, then beat. Add the baking powder and beat again. Use immediately or store in the refrigerator. Makes enough for 1 kg (2 lbs.).

✍STUFFINGS✍

CRANBERRY AND ORANGE STUFFING

250 mL	cranberries, fresh OR frozen	1 cup
30 mL	water	2 Tbsp.
1 medium	orange, peeled and sectioned OR apple, cored and sliced	1 medium
15 mL	lemon juice	1 Tbsp.
30 mL	sugar	2 Tbsp.
30 mL	water	2 Tbsp.
250 mL	soft breadcrumbs	1 cup

Place all ingredients—except bread-crumbs—in a blender and blend until oranges and cranberries are well chopped and mixed. Empty into a pan and cook until tender. Remove from heat, add breadcrumbs, and stir to mix. Makes 500 mL (2 cups). Use to stuff any white-fleshed fillets or as a topping for fish steaks.

HERB AND BREADCRUMB STUFFING

50 mL	butter	¼ cup
75 mL	celery, chopped	⅓ cup
75 mL	onion, chopped	⅓ cup
15 mL	mayonnaise	1 Tbsp.
2 mL	salt	½ tsp.
0.5 mL	pepper	⅛ tsp.
1 mL	tarragon	¼ tsp.
1 mL	thyme	¼ tsp.
250 mL	soft breadcrumbs	1 cup

Melt butter in a frying pan and sauté celery and onion for 3 to 4 minutes until tender-crisp. Remove from heat. In a bowl, combine mayonnaise, salt, pepper, tarragon and thyme, and stir into vegetable mixture. Toss in breadcrumbs. Makes 375 mL (1½ cups). Use to stuff any white-fleshed fillets or whole fish.

LEMON AND RICE STUFFING

75 mL	butter	⅓ cup
250 mL	celery, minced	1 cup
75 mL	onion, minced	⅓ cup
375 mL	cooked rice	1½ cups
50 mL	lemon juice	¼ cup
15 mL	lemon rind, grated	1 Tbsp.
1 mL	thyme	¼ tsp.
10 mL	salt	2 tsp.
0.5 mL	pepper	⅛ tsp.

Melt butter in a frying pan and sauté celery and onion for 3 to 4 minutes until tender-crisp. Add remaining ingredients and mix well. Makes 750 mL (3 cups). Use to stuff fillets or whole fish.

Lemon and Sour Cream Stuffing

50 mL	sour cream	¼ cup
10 mL	lemon rind, grated	2 tsp.
2 mL	salt	½ tsp.
2 mL	paprika	½ tsp.
625 mL	soft bread cubes	2½ cups
30 mL	butter	2 Tbsp.
50 mL	onion, chopped	¼ cup
125 mL	celery, diced	½ cup

Combine in a bowl the sour cream, lemon rind, salt and paprika. Pour over the bread cubes, tossing lightly.

In a frying pan, melt butter and sauté onions and celery until tender. Add to bread cubes and mix well. Makes 0.75 to 1 L (3 to 4 cups). Use to stuff any fillets or whole fish, or as a topping for baked fillets.

Mushroom Stuffing

50 mL	butter	¼ cup
75 mL	celery, chopped	⅓ cup
75 mL	onion, minced	⅓ cup
250 mL	mushrooms, sliced	1 cup
15 mL	parsley, chopped	1 Tbsp.
175 mL	crackers, coarsely crushed	¾ cup
1 mL	poultry seasoning	¼ tsp.
1 mL	fennel OR dried dill weed	¼ tsp.

In a saucepan, melt butter and sauté celery and onion for 3 to 4 minutes until golden brown. Add mushrooms and cook for 2 minutes more. Remove from heat. Stir in remaining ingredients and mix well. Makes 500 to 750 mL (2 to 3 cups).

Use this stuffing for whole baked arctic charr, lake whitefish, salmon, trout or other firm-fleshed fish, or for any rolled fillets. Season cavity of fish with salt and pepper, then stuff.

OYSTER STUFFING

250 g	shucked oysters with liquid	½ pint
125 mL	butter	½ cup
125 mL	celery, diced	½ cup
250 mL	onion, chopped	1 cup
5 mL	salt	1 tsp.
5 mL	poultry seasoning	1 tsp.
2 mL	summer savoury	½ tsp.
4 slices	bread, toasted and cubed	4 slices

Melt butter in a saucepan and sauté celery and onion until tender. Add salt, poultry seasoning, summer savoury and oysters with liquid. Simmer until the edges of the oysters curl. Remove from heat and stir in bread cubes. Makes 0.75 to 1 L (3 to 4 cups). Use for stuffing whole salmon, arctic charr, trout, lake whitefish, or as a stuffing for fillets; excellent for stuffing turkey as well as fish.

SHRIMP STUFFING

113-g can	shrimp	4-oz. can
15 mL	butter	1 Tbsp.
30 mL	onion, minced	2 Tbsp.
50 mL	green pepper, minced	¼ cup
1 mL	sweet basil	¼ tsp.

Drain shrimp, rinse under cold running water, and drain again. Chop up shrimp.

Melt butter in a saucepan and sauté onion and green pepper for 3 to 4 minutes until tender-crisp. Remove from heat. Add shrimp and sweet basil, stirring until well mixed. Makes about 250 mL (1 cup). Use for stuffing any white-fleshed fillets, placing about 30 mL (2 Tbsp.) in each.

SPINACH AND EGG STUFFING

283-g pkg.	frozen spinach	10-oz. pkg.
1	hard-cooked egg, chopped	1
15 mL	lemon juice	1 Tbsp.
2 mL	salt	½ tsp.
0.5 mL	pepper	⅛ tsp.
1 mL	nutmeg	¼ tsp.
250 mL	soft breadcrumbs	1 cup

Cook spinach according to package directions, drain well, and chop finely. Add egg, lemon juice, salt, pepper and nutmeg, then mix well. Add breadcrumbs and toss. Makes 500 mL (2 cups). Use for stuffing whole salmon, arctic charr, trout or lake whitefish, or as a stuffing for fillets.

VEGETABLE STUFFING

30 mL	onion, minced	2 Tbsp.
125 mL	cucumber, peeled, seeded and diced	½ cup
125 mL	tomato, peeled, seeded and chopped	½ cup
50 mL	green pepper, minced	¼ cup
10 mL	lemon juice	2 tsp.
1 mL	salt	¼ tsp.
pinch	pepper	pinch
15 mL	melted butter	1 Tbsp.

Combine all ingredients and mix well. Makes about 300 mL (1¼ cups). Use as a stuffing for any whole fish or fillets.

ᔕSAUCESᔕ

APRICOT-GINGER SAUCE

398-mL can	apricot halves	14-oz. can
5 mL	cornstarch	1 tsp.
15 mL	orange marmalade	1 Tbsp.
5 mL	ginger powder	1 tsp.
15 mL	lemon juice	1 Tbsp.

Drain apricot halves and reserve 15 mL (1 Tbsp.) of juice. Soften cornstarch with the reserved juice.

Put the rest of the ingredients in a blender and blend until smooth (or chop finely). Pour into a saucepan and heat until almost boiling. Add softened cornstarch and heat, stirring, for a further 1 to 2 minutes until sauce is thick and clear. Makes 175 mL (¾ cup). Serve over poached or baked white-fleshed fish fillets or steaks.

BASIC CREAM SAUCE

30 mL	butter	2 Tbsp.
30 mL	flour	2 Tbsp.
250 mL	liquid (milk OR a combination of milk and one of: vegetable stock, fish stock (see index), cream, dry white wine, court bouillon, canned salmon liquid)	1 cup
2 mL	salt	½ tsp.
0.5 mL	white pepper	⅛ tsp.

The flavour of this sauce will differ considerably, depending on the liquid used in its making.

Melt butter in a saucepan, stir in flour, and gradually add liquid. Cook over medium heat, stirring constantly until thickened. Add salt and pepper. Makes about 250 mL (1 cup) of sauce. This sauce and its many variations may be used over fish fillets and steaks, or as a base for many casseroles and soufflés.

VARIATIONS

The consistency of basic cream sauce is easily altered:

Thick cream sauce. Use 50 mL (¼ cup) butter and 50 mL (¼ cup) flour to 250 mL (1 cup) liquid.

Thin cream sauce. Use 15 mL (1 Tbsp.) butter and 15 mL (1 Tbsp.) flour to 250 mL (1 cup) liquid.

Other ingredients may be added to basic cream sauce for additional flavour variations:

Anchovy. Rinse, mash and add 3 anchovy fillets.

Cheese. Add 250 mL (1 cup) grated medium cheddar cheese and a dash of paprika. Stir over low heat until the cheese melts.

Curry. Add 15 mL (1 Tbsp.) curry powder.

Herb. Try adding one of the following: chervil, dill weed, sweet basil, marjoram, fennel, rosemary, tarragon or any other of your favourites that complement fish. Start with 2 mL (½ tsp.) until you reach your individual taste level.

Mustard. Add 2 mL (½ tsp.) dry mustard or 15 mL (1 Tbsp.) prepared mustard.

Parsley-egg. Add one hard-cooked, chopped egg and 15 mL (1 Tbsp.) chopped parsley.

CHINESE SAUCE

30 mL	cornstarch	2 Tbsp.
50 mL	sake OR dry white wine	¼ cup
250 mL	orange juice	1 cup
15 mL	soy sauce	1 Tbsp.
30 mL	sugar	2 Tbsp.
50 mL	vinegar	¼ cup
5 mL	ginger powder	1 tsp.

Soften cornstarch in 30 mL (2 Tbsp.) of the sake. Heat the rest of the sake, orange juice, soy sauce, sugar, vinegar and ginger in a saucepan until almost boiling. Remove from heat and stir in the softened cornstarch. Cook over medium heat, stirring, for a further 1 to 2 minutes until sauce is thickened and clear. Makes about 350 mL (1½ cups). Pour over fillets or steaks and serve immediately.

CHUTNEY SAUCE

175 mL	sour cream	¾ cup
5 mL	curry powder	1 tsp.
50 mL	chutney, chopped or puréed	¼ cup

Mix together all ingredients and chill before serving. Makes 250 mL (1 cup). Good served with cold seafood and shellfish salads.

HAWAIIAN CURRY SAUCE

50 mL	butter	¼ cup
30 mL	onion, minced	2 Tbsp.
30 mL	flour	2 Tbsp.
250 mL	milk	1 cup

5 mL	curry powder	1 tsp.
5 mL	preserved ginger, minced OR	1 tsp.
2 mL	ginger powder	½ tsp.
15 mL	lemon OR lime juice	1 Tbsp.
2 mL	salt	½ tsp.
0.5 mL	pepper	⅛ tsp.
125 mL	coconut, shredded (optional)	½ cup

Melt butter in a saucepan and sauté onion for 2 minutes. Stir in the flour. Add the milk gradually, stirring over medium heat until thickened. Add curry powder, ginger, lemon juice, salt and pepper, stirring for a further 2 minutes. Add more milk if necessary for desired consistency. Coconut may be mixed in with the sauce or sprinkled on top when served. Makes 500 mL (2 cups). This sauce is good with shrimp or crab.

Hollandaise Sauce

125 mL	butter	½ cup
3	egg yolks	3
30 mL	lemon juice	2 Tbsp.
1 mL	salt	¼ tsp.
pinch	cayenne pepper	pinch
125 mL	water	½ cup

Melt butter in a saucepan but do not let brown.

Put egg yolks, lemon juice, salt and cayenne into blender container. Run on low speed for 30 seconds. Add water and run on low speed for a further 30 seconds. Put blender on high speed and pour in melted butter in a thin, steady stream. Continue beating until all the melted butter is blended. Transfer to a double boiler and heat over hot water, stirring continuously until thickened. Do not let boil. Makes 250 mL (1 cup). Serve immediately over or with any white-fleshed fish.

LEMON SAUCE

30 mL	butter	2 Tbsp.
30 mL	flour	2 Tbsp.
250 mL	court bouillon (see index) OR chicken bouillon	1 cup
	(may include up to 125 mL (½ cup) white wine)	
30 mL	lemon juice	2 Tbsp.
2 mL	salt	½ tsp.
0.5 mL	dried dill weed	⅛ tsp.

Melt butter in a saucepan, then add flour and court bouillon, stirring over medium heat until thickened. Add lemon juice, salt and dill. Cook over medium heat, stirring, for 2 minutes longer. Makes 250 mL (1 cup). Serve hot over any white-fleshed fillets or steaks.

MOCK HOLLANDAISE SAUCE

250 mL	basic cream sauce (see index)	1 cup
500 mL	mayonnaise	2 cups
15 mL	lemon juice	1 Tbsp.
2 drops	Tabasco sauce	2 drops
	salt to taste	

To basic cream sauce, add rest of the ingredients, while stirring over medium heat. Makes 750 mL (3 cups). Serve hot.

RICHELIEU SAUCE

250 mL	mayonnaise	1 cup
50 mL	sour cream	¼ cup
30 mL	lemon juice	2 Tbsp.
5 mL	lemon rind, grated	1 tsp.
2 mL	Worcestershire sauce	½ tsp.

Mix all ingredients together and chill before serving. Makes 350 mL (1½ cups). Serve with any cold fish or shellfish.

SEAFOOD COCKTAIL SAUCE NO. 1

125 mL	chili sauce	½ cup
75 mL	ketchup	⅓ cup
15 mL	horseradish	1 Tbsp.
7 mL	Worcestershire sauce	1½ tsp.

Mix all ingredients together and chill before serving. Makes 250 mL (1 cup). Serve with cold crab, shrimp, lobster, clams or mussels.

SEAFOOD COCKTAIL SAUCE NO. 2

125 mL	chili sauce	½ cup
50 mL	lemon juice	¼ cup
15 mL	vinegar	1 Tbsp.
15 mL	Worcestershire sauce	1 Tbsp.
30 mL	celery, minced	2 Tbsp.
30 mL	onion, minced	2 Tbsp.
15 mL	parsley, chopped	1 Tbsp.
2 drops	Tabasco sauce	2 drops

Combine all ingedients and chill before serving. Makes 250 mL (1 cup). Serve with cold shellfish.

SHERRY-MUSHROOM CREAM SAUCE

30 mL	butter	2 Tbsp.
375 mL	mushrooms, sliced	1½ cups
30 mL	flour	2 Tbsp.
250 mL	light cream	1 cup
30 mL	whipping cream	2 Tbsp.
30 mL	sherry	2 Tbsp.
	salt and pepper	

Melt the butter in a saucepan and sauté mushrooms for 2 to 3 minutes. Stir in flour, then gradually pour in the light cream, stirring continuously over medium heat until thickened. Stir in the whipping cream and sherry, then season with salt and pepper to taste. Makes about 675 mL (2½ cups). Serve hot with fish fillets or steaks.

TARTARE SAUCE

5 mL	onion, minced	1 tsp.
10 mL	capers, minced	2 tsp.
10 mL	sweet pickle, minced	2 tsp.
15 mL	parsley, minced	1 Tbsp.
10 mL	green olives, chopped	2 tsp.
175 mL	mayonnaise	¾ cup
15 mL	tarragon OR wine vinegar	1 Tbsp.

Mix all ingredients together and chill before serving. Makes 175 mL (¾ cup). Excellent with deep-fried or pan-fried fish or shellfish.

ᏝSALAD DRESSINGSᏝ

CHIVE DRESSING

250 mL	plain yogurt	1 cup
5 mL	lemon juice	1 tsp.
5 mL	seasoned salt	1 tsp.
15 mL	chives, finely snipped OR	1 Tbsp.
	green onion, minced	

Combine all ingredients and mix well. Chill before serving. Makes 250 mL (1 cup). Serve with cold fish.

CHUTNEY DRESSING

15 mL	mayonnaise	1 Tbsp.
125 mL	sour cream	½ cup
30 mL	Major Grey's chutney	2 Tbsp.
7 mL	lemon juice	1½ tsp.
2 mL	onion, minced	½ tsp.

Mix all ingredients together and chill for one hour before serving. Makes 175 mL (¾ cup). Serve with a fish or shellfish and fruit salad combination.

FRENCH DRESSING

175 mL	olive OR salad oil	¾ cup
50 mL	cider OR wine vinegar	¼ cup
2 mL	salt	½ tsp.
0.5 mL	freshly ground pepper	⅛ tsp.

Measure all ingredients into a covered jar and shake well. Refrigerate until ready to serve. Shake well again before serving. Makes 250 mL (1 cup). Use on any fish or shellfish salad.

VARIATIONS

Other ingredients may be added to vary the flavour:

Garlic. Add 1 clove of crushed garlic to the basic recipe and shake well.
Herb. Add 10 to 15 mL (2 to 3 tsp.) chopped parsley and 2 mL (½ tsp.) tarragon to the basic recipe and shake well.

FRENCH-STYLE DRESSING

2 mL	gelatin	½ tsp.
15 mL	cold water	1 Tbsp.
125 mL	boiling water	½ cup
15 mL	sugar	1 Tbsp.
5 mL	salt	1 tsp.
125 mL	lemon juice	½ cup
1 mL	onion juice	¼ tsp.
0.5 mL	pepper	⅛ tsp.
few grains	cayenne pepper	few grains

In a 500 mL (1 pt.) jar, soften gelatin in cold water. Pour in the boiling water, cover jar, and shake well. Add all the remaining ingredients, cover, and shake until all ingredients are dissolved. Chill for several hours before using. Makes 250 mL (1 cup). Use on any fish or shellfish salad.

HERB AND COTTAGE CHEESE DRESSING

250 mL	dry cottage cheese	1 cup
15 mL	milk	1 Tbsp.
30 mL	green onion, chopped	2 Tbsp.
15 mL	lemon juice	1 Tbsp.
1 mL	salt	¼ tsp.
0.5 mL	pepper	⅛ tsp.
2 mL	fresh dill, minced OR	½ tsp.
0.5 mL	dried dill weed	⅛ tsp.
few drops	Tabasco sauce	few drops

Place all ingredients in a blender and beat until creamy-smooth, or whip the cottage cheese with milk until creamy, then add the remaining ingredients and mix. Chill for several hours before serving. Makes 250 mL (1 cup). Use on any fish or shellfish salad.

LOUIS DRESSING

250 mL	mayonnaise	1 cup
50 mL	French dressing (see index)	¼ cup
175 mL	chili sauce	¾ cup
30 mL	onion, minced	2 Tbsp.
5 mL	horseradish	1 tsp.
5 mL	Worcestershire sauce	1 tsp.

Mix all ingredients together well and chill before serving. Makes 500 mL (2 cups). This dressing goes well with crab, lobster and shrimp.

LOW-CALORIE MAYONNAISE

7 mL	sugar	1½ tsp.
7 mL	dry mustard	1½ tsp.
2 mL	salt	½ tsp.
0.5 mL	paprika	⅛ tsp.
7 mL	cornstarch	1½ tsp.

1	egg, lightly beaten	1
125 mL	buttermilk	½ cup
15 mL	melted butter	1 Tbsp.
50 mL	vinegar	¼ cup

In the top of a double-boiler, mix together the dry ingredients. Beat in the egg and buttermilk until smooth. Cook, beating or stirring over hot water, until mixture begins to thicken. Add melted butter and vinegar gradually, beating well after each addition. Remove from heat, cool, and chill before serving. Makes 175 mL (¾ cup). Serve on any fish or shellfish salad.

LOW-CALORIE TOMATO DRESSING

125 mL	tomato juice	½ cup
30 mL	salad oil	2 Tbsp.
30 mL	lemon juice	2 Tbsp.
5 mL	onion, grated	1 tsp.
5 mL	salt	1 tsp.
2 mL	dry mustard	½ tsp.

Combine all ingredients. Beat well with a wire whisk or shake in a tightly covered jar. Chill before using. Makes 175 mL (¾ cup). Serve on any fish or shellfish salad.

ORANGE AND SPICE DRESSING

15 mL	mayonnaise	1 Tbsp.
125 mL	sour cream OR plain yogurt	½ cup
5 mL	honey	1 tsp.
15 mL	concentrated frozen orange juice	1 Tbsp.
1 mL	ginger powder	¼ tsp.
1 mL	cinnamon	¼ tsp.

Mix all ingredients together and chill before using. Makes 175 mL (¾ cup). Serve on any fish or shellfish and fruit salad combination.

ᔯINDEXᔮ

Options appear in brackets. Page numbers that refer to illustrations are in **bold** type.